COCOA WOMAN

*a narrative about cocoa estate culture
in the British West Indies*

JOHNNY COOMANSINGH

Ordering Information:

For orders and inquiries, please contact:
1-888-375-9818
www.toplinkpublishing.com
bookorder@toplinkpublishing.com

Printed in the United States of America

DEDICATION

This book is dedicated to my grandson, Jace Jessel Coomansingh

PREFACE

AGAINST THE BACKGROUND of colonial domination and exploitation in Trinidad and Tobago, *Cocoa Woman:* seeks to uncover a selection of experiences Jonjon endured with Neeta his godmother. In her quest to amass a vast fortune, Jonjon literally became a child slave. This is a glad story, but yet a sad story about a childless woman, a wife, and a godmother who fought the world to gain wealth in whatever way she could. In her economic struggle, she rallied tooth and nail, even against her husband, her in-laws, relatives, and neighbors to avariciously scrape up every black penny to generate a fortune; a fortune she left without a last will and testament. Who eventually ended up with the money, house, and land, is quite a bit of intrigue; many questions, no answers. *Cocoa Woman* seeks to provide a description of the play and interplay of personalities who seemingly kept their eyes on the money. The scene is partially set on Oropouche Road, Sangre Grande, and Kowlessur Road in the village of Sangre Chiquito, Trinidad.

Reliving some events during a tiny part of his childhood Jonjon was of the view that he could have confided in everyone with whom he came into contact. In his simple childishness he also thought that everyone he encountered genuinely cared. Jonjon was so very wrong; so naïve. He was fair game to be used, abused and somewhat confused by people he loved and trusted. In this story, he became a minion, a cog in the wheel of a multinational cocoa production syndicate. The drive to produce excesses of export quality cocoa beans in Trinidad and Tobago became an obsession. There was much money to be made; cocoa was king. Child slave labor was imperceptibly woven into the tapestry and it seemed that many producers thought that this form of labor was acceptable. And it was the poorer "class" of people and their children who suffered.

Although Neeta was one of the less significant cocoa producers in Trinidad, she stopped at nothing to exploit and sometimes even abuse anyone she could capture in her clutches; anyone at all. She was an expert in wheedling and sweet-talking, and without conscience, lured people into her web. Being fatherless and struggling to survive, it was easy for her to capture, fool, and manipulate poor children like Jonjon. There were others whom she manipulated at will to do her bidding. Quite bizarre and mind-boggling was the power she had over her "captives." There were people who believed that the food she offered was laced with potions and charms. Jonjon is not certain about what these people assumed. Nevertheless, it is worth a bit of research. All he knows is that she was a great cook, her food was mouthwatering, and there was always something there for him to consume.

Cocoa Woman speaks to the discomfort, the pain, the suffering, and what Jonjon now speculates to be the abuse he endured while spending weekends and school vacations on Neeta's cocoa plantation. In retrospect, it was nothing short of child slave labor. In some way, Jonjon feels that he stomached "slave labor" just because he received a little morsel to eat. The abuse was much more than just physical. Unknowingly, he suffered mental as well as psychological abuse.

There is a dichotomy that exists when someone knows what the right thing to do is and somebody that they love and respect tells them that it is okay, for example, to steal. How to fight back against the flood of her dishonesty was his predicament. Jonjon was misled in so many ways. The confusion that reigned in his mind was debilitating. *Cocoa Woman* goes deep into the annals of a history that Jonjon would prefer to forget; but forget, he can't.

Cocoa Woman is poignant, direct and to the point. It unleashes the spirit of the cocoa field, and fully exposes the daily menial rounds of production, the never-ending chores, the angst, "deadlines," language idioms, village bacchanal, beliefs, cuisine, artefacts, folkways, and foibles that intertwined to constitute cocoa estate culture. Although this narrative is true, the author has elected to use fictitious names and labels to protect the identity of the various persons mentioned. As far as Jonjon can recall, the three major players, in the story are deceased *Neeta*-his godmother, *Quero* her taxi-driver husband, and *Francois Dohfeh*, the old patois speaking man who lived "up di hill" on Kowlessur Road. Other actors are mentioned, also with fictitious names. For whatever reason, it was Jonjon's father who prescribed the label "Quero" to Neeta's husband. From what Jonjon remembered, Quero was a name he was not too happy about.

CHAPTER ONE

*If chocolate is considered to be the "food of the
gods" then there are some seriously evil and
terrible gods in the cocoa business.*

"Caught in the web..."

EXCRUCIATING PAIN UNDER Jonjon's fingernails accompanied by swollen throbbing fingers was the net effect after a day of cocoa bean extraction from the never-ending pile of ripe cocoa pods. As streaks of filtered sunlight danced on the glistening red, yellow, and orange colored pods, the enormous heaps presented a prosperous sight indeed to the cocoa entrepreneur; it was money! The heaps were sometimes four or five times the size of the heap shown in Figure 1.

In the hot and humid, mosquito-infested cocoa field, Jonjon was directed to sit around immense heaps of cocoa pods scattered throughout the 20-acre field while Neeta, his godmother, filled a large cocoa basket in front of him with cracked, half-opened pods. With deft speed, and beads of perspiration pouring down her face, she did not even flinch to brush off a mosquito. The "cracker-dull," a small sharp steel blade about 8-12 inches long fitted with a short, cloth-wound, wooden handle, found its mark on the large multicolored pods. This was the pod cracking process.

Figure 1. A heap of ripe cocoa pods
(Photo credits Leon Granger, 2015. Used with permission)

Cracking or breaking cocoa is an art where hand and eye coordination is tuned to its finest. This work necessitates exacting speed and unison; yes, much experience in this type of activity is required lest fingers slip silently away after contact with the blade. The cracker-dull becomes sharper with each pod that is broken--razor sharp. Neeta was a master cocoa "cracker" who artfully crammed the baskets around the heap faster than you could ever clean out the pods. Without even raising her head, she never missed a basket. In her mind was a map of all the baskets that were situated around the heap. Not one slimy cocoa bean ever hit the ground as she piled to capacity everyone's basket around the heap.

Removing cocoa beans from the ripe pods was not a task Jonjon relished. He detested this grueling and miserable chore. No ten or eleven-year old boy likes such tedium, restriction, regimentation, and rigor, but such was Jonjon's plight. He had no choice in this part of his life. This cocoa bean removal activity was one of the most disgusting aspects of work in the cocoa field that he experienced. The sticky, semi-acid, semi-sweet cocoa juice that inundated his hands and fingers did not offer any assistance to the hurried, and somewhat interminable routine.

Digging in with fingertips inside the pods invariably caused bits of the pod lining or membrane to lodge under Jonjon's fingernails. The idea was to have all the pods cleaned out without the accumulation of *la peau*, (French meaning *skin*) the uncleaned broken pods hidden under a layer of fresh slimy beans. If the la peau was too much to contend with in the basket, there were times when the broken pods would be thrown onto banana leaves spread out on the ground. It was worse when the pods were black or half rotted.

Apart from the putrid, nauseating smell of the black pods, all manner of little crawling, strange looking, frightful, creepy insects and arthropods would be present inside the pods. Jonjon abhorred the rotted pods as well as the pesky mosquitoes that he sought to slay behind his ears with hands slathered in cocoa juice. The throbbing pain in his fingers the following day was physical torment as he sat ruminating around the huge pile of cocoa pods in the field. When will this cocoa-cracking activity end? What was the best plan to escape this experience? Immersion of his hands at the close of the day in warm salty water to ease the agony was welcomed. The soothing effect of salt water would last for a moment, but the cycle of pain started once more during the cocoa bean extraction activity the next day around the heaps of cocoa.

Without question; the object of "cracking cocoa" was to bring in the cocoa crop as quickly as possible. Leaving the harvested cocoa pods too long in large piles on the ground in the field could result in damage to the quality of the beans. As Jonjon surmised, the people who were in control of the world cocoa market were fussy, inflexible, and somewhat arrogant; at least so he was told.

From what he witnessed, cocoa producers in Trinidad walked a very thin and complex line to meet the strict requirements of producing the right kind of cocoa beans for the world market. It was obvious that producers struggled to fulfill the stringent conditions necessary to fetch a higher price for their beans. Beans with the incorrect moisture content or beans that exhibited poor quality or *flot* or empty beans, could mean reduced payments or no income at all. The local buyers paid very little if cocoa beans were flattened, or flot. In *patois*, this was labeled *passé*. (past the prime; faded or aged, from old French "passer" to pass).

Cocoa production in Trinidad was concerned with the demands to satisfy the palate of a chocolate-hungry external market. Somehow, and for whatever reasons, Jonjon became ensnared, caught in the international web of cocoa production-- a web that was difficult to escape. He was trapped. Jonjon was just a child, not more than ten or eleven years old, yet he was made to do hard, tedious work, to sweat, to experience untold pain and discomfort in a system that could not care about anyone.

Did anyone seek to understand whose child was made to suffer in the cocoa fields of Trinidad? If chocolate was considered to be the "food of the gods" then there were some seriously evil gods in the cocoa business. How did Jonjon come to be sweating and toiling in his godmother's cocoa field doing such menial tasks? Furnishing a few facts about how and why she came to be a small cocoa proprietor on Kowlessur Road in Sangre Chiquito will serve to provide an answer.

Figure 2. A relic from the Santa Estrella Cocoa estate,
probably the former manager's residence.
(Photo by author, 2015)

Located at the corner between the Manzanilla Road, (a section of the Eastern Main Road (EMR), Sangre Chiquito and Kowlessur Road is one of the great houses (Figure. 2) constructed when cocoa production was at its all-time high. Even now, there is no actual point of focus that serves as the geographic center of the village of Sangre Chiquito. This house remains as an icon to the history of cocoa production in the area and the overlords who took up residence in Sangre Chiquito. Owned by an East Indian family, to the west of this house, on the other side of Kowlessur Road, there once was a grocery store where Jonjon's godmother purchased her grocery items. Sangre Chiquito used to be a tiny village with an agrarian lifestyle. However, cocoa production in this village has been severely reduced; the essence of real rural living is now a thing of the past.

Figure 3. A view of the Eastern Main Road and a built up area in Sangre Chiquito today. (Photograph by author, 2015).

Over time, several business places were erected including hardware stores, groceries, and chicken production farms. A home for poor and destitute children with a Christian orientation was also built and functioned for quite a few years. The children's home is now defunct as well as one of the hardware stores and a couple of grocery stores. A few auto-mechanic and collision auto body shops are present in the village. Except for the Presbyterian elementary school (Figure 4) and the Presbyterian Church situated at the crest of the hill above Gadjadar Road, which could probably serve as the focal point, the village is basically a row of houses and small business enterprises, such as "rum shops" and grocery stores constructed along both sides of the Manzanilla Road (Eastern Main Road). Included in its planning, Sangre Chiquito boasts of a recreation ground or facility where cricket, basketball, and football are played. The field also caters for community gatherings, and track and field games. Many of the shops and groceries serve as supply stores for beachgoers who travel to the Manzanilla Beach just about four miles east. Fruit vendors also dot the roadsides with whatever fruit is in season, including mango, ripe bananas, *pommerac, kashema,* and *pommecythere.* Green coconuts savored for the good, cool and healthy coconut water are always available. Sangre Chiquito to the east is considered an extension of Sangre Grande, which is about four miles west.

Figure 4. The Sangre Chiquito Presbyterian Elementary School
(Photo by author, 201

In the era when cocoa was "king" (mainstay economic crop) in Trinidad and Tobago, Sangre Grande was more or less sufficiently developed as the center of cocoa production in the east. Remnants of this epoch can still be seen in the photograph of the cocoa store (Figure 5) situated on the Eastern Main Road, in Sangre Grande. Legend has it that the Spanish explorers named the two towns because of the color of the water in both the Cunapo River that passes through Sangre Grande, and the smaller Sangre Chiquito River that flows further east.

Figure 5. The Bidaisee Cocoa Store on Eastern Main Road, Sangre Grande (Photo by author, 2008)

They found that the waters in both rivers looked like blood only to discover that certain flowers that fell into the water coupled with the red sand that flowed in the rivers influenced the color of the water. Who knows for sure if this "flower" and "red sand" story is true? There is however another story to the Spanish toponyms given to these towns. There is the claim by many Trinidadian historians and raconteurs that there were two violent and bloody clashes between the Spanish conquerors and the Native Amerindians. One of the battles waged in Sangre Grande where there was much bloodshed and the other about four miles east where there was little bloodshed, hence the names Sangre Grande and Sangre Chiquito. The history about these toponyms is nonetheless lost in the mists of time. Incidentally, the central business district (CBD) in Sangre Grande is referred to as Cunapo or colloquially, as "Cunaps."

Occupation of what is now Sangre Chiquito began with the Amerindians who arrived and settled several centuries before the Spanish intruders. Following the Spanish were African slaves who were supplanted by South Asian (East Indian) indentured immigrants of the British Crown during the early 19th century. These indentured migrants found work as laborers on sugar cane plantations and cocoa estates. One of the cocoa estates where they found work was the Santa Estrella cocoa estate.

Joining the East Indian population thereafter were a small number of Venezuelans commonly referred to as *Cocoa Panyols* (payol). Even today, people who look like those of Spanish or Portuguese (fair-skinned) extract are still called *payol* in Trinidad and Tobago. Some are also referred to as *Bakra-Johnny*. It is thought that Bakra-Johnny was originally "Backrow Johnny" where poor whites had to sit in church on Sunday in the old time days. The upper class sat to the front and the poor whites had to sit in the back rows. Over time, it was shortened to "Bakra Johnny." As a Hispanic ethnicity, the Cocoa Panyol is a mixture of Amerindian, African, and European (possibly Iberian) races. Probably derived from "patois" or broken Spanish, "Espanol," or "espagnol," the term Panyol refers to a group of people who are associated with cocoa production in Trinidad.

The mixture of ethnicities brought with them their cultural baggage. Inclusive in this baggage were their religious persuasions, plants, seeds, language, dress, art, music, cuisine, and magic. Nevertheless, there were Christian missionaries, including Dr. John Morton who directly and indirectly proselytized the indentured East Indians. Converting to the Canadian Presbyterian way of life were quite a few of the indentured workers.

The work of the Presbyterian Church eventually blossomed into the establishment of the Sangre Chiquito Canadian Mission School for Indians in the year 1891, the first Presbyterian school to be built in the northeastern sector of Trinidad. The institution was later rebuilt and renamed Sangre Chiquito Presbyterian School. A little later, a Presbyterian church was erected. In 1920, a family related to Juan Vincente Gomez Chacon, a former dictator from Venezuela, arrived in Sangre Chiquito. With the arrival of these colonists, cultural, physical, and economic changes occurred in rapid succession on the landscape. These changes have remained until the present time.

The supposedly wealthy family headed by Colmenares Pacheco, a Venezuelan army general, settled on the Santa Estrella cocoa estate. This 900-acre parcel of land was formerly owned by the Gransaul and Murray families. In a joint venture, Pacheco and his brother-in-law Gomez (The Tyrant of the Andes) bought the Santa Estrella Estate occupying the lands between Kowlessur and Gadjadar Roads.

Figure 6. The Santa Estrella Cocoa Estate great house
where Pacheco resided (Photo by author, 2015)

In the year 1924, they erected immense and elaborate houses to really establish themselves on what is now known as the Eastern Main Road (EMR). Built with Spanish styled architecture inclusive of wrap around verandahs, tiled hipped roofs, and strong thick walls, these houses are still standing and functional.

They are icons that bear witness to the history of cocoa plantation life; literal showpieces of Trinidadian heritage. On the opposite side of the EMR the cocoa entrepreneurs built the estate office, stables, cocoa drying houses, and the cocoa fermentation box or sweat box. The family lived in the house as shown in Figure 6 while the estate manager occupied the other (Figure 2) located adjacent to Kowlessur Road. General Pacheco died in 1953 and as far as everyone could remember, the name of the estate was known as "Pacheco Estate." People in Sangre Chiquito and elsewhere seldom refer to the name "Santa Estrella." Without question, the Santa Estrella estate became the hub of economic activity, and invariably served as the cultural center of village activities. Santa Estrella employed most of the laborers in the village and fostered opportunities for home ownership among its residents. It is almost certain that the Cocoa Panyols introduced Parranda (Parang) to Sangre Chiquito in their celebration of Christmas.

The mention of parang necessitates an explanation of what comprises this activity. Parang is basically associated with feting and merrymaking at Christmastime. Small groups of villagers comprising about four or five men, the *paranderos*, would sometimes engage in an *aparrandaat* at festive events, for example, a baby's christening or a person's birthday. Singing Spanish ballads at such celebrations accompanied with musical instruments gave rise to a jovial atmosphere; pure merriment. Such instruments included the *cuatro* (small four-stringed instrument derived from the Portuguese *cavaquinho*), a salt box base, a pair of *maracas* or *shac-shac* and maybe a fiddle and a mandolin. The cuatro (Figure 7) is considered to be the national instrument of Venezuela. There are claims that the parang practiced in Trinidad and Tobago today came from Venezuela, in the form known as *parranda navidena* or "Christmas parang."

Figure 7. What a cuatro looks like (Photo by author, 2014)

With just seven miles east across the Gulf of Paria, the relative location of Trinidad to Venezuela probably encouraged the acceptance and growth of parang with all its folkloric trappings into Trinidad. It is clear, because of proximity, that cultural exchanges were attributable to the constant interaction between the island and the South American mainland. Around Christmastime, the parang musical art-form envelops the landscape. Who brought the parang is still uncertain. Was it the "cocoa panyols" or the Spanish colonists (1498-1797)? No one can really give an exact and conclusive answer as to who brought the parang. Nevertheless, parang is now widespread on the cultural landscape of Trinidad and Tobago.

Citing a snippet of an article produced by the Trinidad and Tobago National Library (*www.nalis.gov.tt*) "...parang has been called a fusion of the deep spiritual aspirations of the Spanish people and the unfettered joyfulness of the Amerindian and African cultures." Regardless of its origins, style, instruments, people, songs, and performance format, parang found its way among the estate workers in Sangre Grande and Sangre Chiquito. Moreover, parang has always been an activity laced with singing, merriment, instrumentalists, dancing, and obviously, the preparation and sharing of special food and drink. Nevertheless, all good things must come to an end. The melodious tones of men and women in an exultant and sweet parang wafting on the rural midnight air among the workers gradually came to a hush. Many of the estate barracks on the plantation where the workers lived were soon vacated. There was trouble on the international cocoa market. Without a means of earning a daily wage, laborers left. As with every commodity on the world market, supply and demand affect prices.

Cocoa production in Trinidad remained at an all-time high, even to point where Trinidad was the third largest producer of cocoa in the world after Ecuador and Venezuela. Trinidad did not remain at that high point for long. Serious labor shortages and soft prices for cocoa beans worked in tandem to reduce supply.

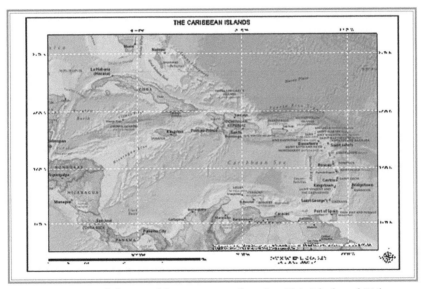

Map 1. Map of the Caribbean region showing Trinidad and Tobago (Cartographer: Luke Gaugler. Used with permission).

Since it was not economically feasible anymore to produce cocoa on the Santa Estrella estate, an idea to subdivide the estate became an imperative. Ten-acre plots were sold to tenants who previously had leases on the land. Somehow, Jonjon's godmother, during the mid-1960s, came into ownership of part of the Pacheco Estate, approximately 20 acres at the three-quarter mile mark on Kowlessur Road. With the acquisition and management of this parcel of land, she became, in every way possible, what one could label as a *cocoa woman*. Something drove her into the cocoa field.

What was it that drove Neeta to want to own a cocoa plantation? Was she tired of rebuff and denigration from the neighbors? Was there some form of competitive spirit in her psyche to raise herself above her peers or her husband and his family? It could have been a dream she had when she was a child. Who knows? Her entire life was built around cocoa estate culture. To inherit or acquire a cocoa plantation was, for all wants and purposes, a dream come true. In light of her new land acquisition, Neeta changed her persona and exchanged her lady-like attire for that of blue dock pants, a long-sleeved khaki shirt, a head tie, and a pair of tall top rubber boots (Wellintons). Her tool shed would now be equipped with a cocoa rod (gullet), a *poinyah* a cracker-dull, and a *louchet*. Soon enough she would move from the comforts of her home at Oropouche Road. A new road formed in her mind.

CHAPTER TWO

*"The road is always there. The question is whether
we will choose the path set before us."*

Interpreting what you think you saw...

OROPOUCHE ROAD IN Sangre Grande, Trinidad, held a very significant place in the life of Jonjon and his family. On this road he came to know Neeta, his godmother, Aunty Dee, his father's Grenadian-born aunt, Uncle Harro her husband, her six grown children, and the three grandchildren that lived in her house. Imperceptible as it may seem, the influences exerted on Jonjon and his three smaller siblings by these individuals forms part of this story and shows how he came to be in the "grips" of the *Cocoa Woman*. Almost every time he visited his godmother there was a constant pulling and tugging at his heart strings. There was an incessant banter about him between Neeta and his second cousins who lived on the adjacent allotment. Everyone seemed to voice their opinion about him and his family. A never-ending fight between them contended for his "soul." Whom should he believe? Who was telling the truth? How does he make a decision? To whom should he yield his allegiance? His confusion was a living nightmare.

Neeta did not get the best of accolades and applause from her neighbors. None of them really respected or truly appreciated her. Jonjon observed that there was a definite tension between all the people in Neeta's neighborhood. It seemed that nobody trusted anyone. In the micro-culture that existed around Neeta there were people of various religious persuasions, including Roman Catholics, Seventh Day Adventists, Spiritual Baptists, Gospel Hall Brethren, Muslims, and Hindus. Each one had their say about everyone else about who was nasty, who was living and cohabiting with whose man or woman, and who was "social," which actually meant that such people were anti-social. Minding each other's business was the order of the day and those who taught themselves "saved" from sin sought to pronounce judgement on the "sinners' in the neighborhood. Some of them looked each other in the eye without uttering a greeting, not even saying "Good morning." Why was this so? The atmosphere in Neeta's "village" was laced with snobbishness, envy, and jealousy.

Well, it must be recorded that Aunty Dee was well-known for her constant denigration of all and sundry in her immediate environs. Jonjon was of the view that she embraced racist views. She came from Grenada where her family was thought to be part of the "upper class," with attendant house servants, cooks, and stable boys. Her racist attitude was deplorable. Anyone she disliked was labeled as a "common class" person, and she kept repeating in Jonjon's ears her infamous words: "common class people." Aunty Dee "sifted" people in the neighborhood and kept talking all day about the reason why they were common class people; she was right, and her religion was God's way. She felt that she was a cut above the rest of the people who resided on Oropouche Road.

Aunty Dee blathered all day long. Because of her incessant chatter, Aunty Dee received the label "Cockot," the name normally given to the green Amazonian parrots that people keep as pets in Trinidad. Jonjon made her out to be a cultural imperialist; it was her way or the highway. All the children called her Cockot. Her demanding, feisty, dogmatic, and ritualistic ways did not contribute to the health of the neighborhood. One Christmastime Jonjon felt her denial of him. She ignored him during a Christmas tree party for the children in the area. She did not pay him any attention. He never forgot how she treated him. It was quite apparent that Aunty Dee was more interested in the children who attended her Sunday School class. She did not show impartiality on that occasion, but yet bad-mouthed and condemned Neeta who was her next-door "neighbor." Cockot was set in her ways and no one could tell her differently.

Aunty Dee's self-righteous attitude was appalling. She yapped all day about "salvation" and her belief in God but did not exhibit the true virtues of Christianity. Even though they were members of the same church and drank communion wine from the same chalice, poor, old Uncle Harro received the worst tongue lashings from Aunty Dee. Jonjon never heard them speaking to each other, but Aunty Dee berated him by "dropping" her words of hate. Despite Aunty Dee's vitriol, Uncle Harro never replied. He proved to be a man of great patience and prayer.

Whenever Jonjon and his younger siblings visited Aunty Dee they would go upstairs to quickly greet her and leave. The children did not like to have too long a stay around her. Aunty Dee's judgmental attitude was not something they preferred to experience. However, there was one evening when the children visited her and to their surprise, Aunty Dee started singing a song: "I know what you will like, like, I know what you will like, like." So what was the surprise? It was a lump of bluish, black sweet potato pone baked in a five pound size Norwegian butter tin. This sweetmeat did not look at all pleasing or palatable to Jonjon and his little sisters. Although Aunty Dee insisted that they should have some of her precious pone, the children hurriedly gave to her a cock-and-bull excuse and fled the scene. For the rest of the evening they kept far from Aunty Dee's sight. Jonjon had to deal with all the influencers around him. There were so many questions and so few were the answers.

In Jonjon's search for the answers to his questions, a small lesson in cultural geography was required. Jonjon was led to believe that a better understanding of people and their behaviors had much to do with their point of origin, the customs they observed, and the cultural baggage they lugged from place to place. Moreover, their cultural values, *viz-a-viz*, religious belief, in no small way, provided a prop, a kind of status-oriented concept for their attitude to other people who do not fall within the sphere of their understanding or interpretation of the world. So an introduction to Oropouche Road and an insight into Jonjon's beginnings has become a necessity.

Heading east on the Eastern Main Road (a.k.a Manzanilla Road), Oropouche Road is the third road on the left after the Sangre Grande Police Station situated at the roundabout. The roundabout controls traffic from Ojoe, Foster, and Toco roads as they merge onto the Eastern Main Road. About half of a mile into Oropouche Road was, for all wants and purposes, Jonjon's point of emergence. Jonjon was told that he was born in a house known as "Martin House," an adobe structure without a ceiling. His father, a cabinet maker/carpenter was a back-slidden Seventh Day Adventist and his mother a nominal Roman Catholic. So his upbringing was a mixture of Adventism and Catholicism. Although he was christened in the Roman Catholic Church, Jonjon never attended church because of his father's influence in the home. He was the last child in his family to be christened under Roman Catholic rites. Before him were five children, three brothers and two sisters and after him were three, two sisters and one brother. A few years later his family moseyed a little farther up Oropouche Road to another adobe house, which he came to know as "Miss John House."

Surrounded by cocoa, coffee, banana, and immortelle trees with a short dirt track from the main road, Miss John House also had a corrugated galvanized steel roof without a ceiling. Rain falling on the roof at nights was a lullaby. We all loved the rain during the night, except for the mud that formed in the track to the house the next morning. Along the track were several large clumps of Christmas palms growing in the front yard. These palms cast long dark shadows on moonlit nights. Jonjon's uncle, his father's brother, used to hide behind these palm trees at night to frighten his elder sisters and brothers.

It is the assumption that an agrarian lifestyle settlement on Oropouche Road began with people who leased roadside plots of land from the large land holdings owned by the Peetams, an East Indian family. All of them came with their religious belief, language, and folkways, and of course, their hopes and dreams. Jonjon remembers well Mrs. Mungool, the loud and noisy lady who prattled and quarreled all day, and certainly, a part of the night. For the way she carried on in the village, Jonjon assumed that this lady had a motor in her mouth. She lived obliquely opposite to Neeta. Neeta never had anything good to say about Mrs. Mungool or her children. In fact, Neeta was a bit apprehensive about Mrs. Mungool's children; she did not like them around. During Jonjon's early years, cocoa, coffee, citrus, and banana production were in full production along the Oropouche Road. Trinidad was just another dependency in the British Empire where such crops were raised to furnish the tables of the elite in Europe. Oropouche Road went straight through to the village of Fishing Pond, the home of the Non Pareil Estate where at one time, rubber was produced.

Uncle Harro had a mixed acreage of cocoa, coffee, and banana trees further up on Oropouche Road, a couple miles from the village of Fishing Pond. Uncle Harro was a quiet, gentle, peaceful man who seldom spoke, but his love for us was overwhelming. Rain or shine, Jonjon remembers that Uncle Harro used to board the six o'clock Public Transport Service Corporation (PTSC) bus every morning in front of the house, to go work on his small plantation. Uncle Harro stayed there all day and returned with the last bus for the evening.

At that time, Oropouche Road did not have a sidewalk or street lighting. Although there were few vehicles on the road, an individual still had to take particular notice when walking along the road at nights. Snakes could be anywhere in the bushes that fringed the roadway. Halfway between Jonjon's home (Miss John house) and Neeta's house there was a wide ravine that drained a low-lying area of the lands that belonged to the Peetams who lived higher up Oropouche Road. Over this ravine was a concrete bridge with its outdated rails painted in black and white.

Crossing this bridge during the day was not at all problematic. The road was well-paved with asphalt. At nights however, there was a bit of trepidation in passing the bridge on the way home. The low-lying, lagoon area surrounding the bridge would sometime fog over, making the area look a little more eerie. The cold, damp, and sinister feeling of the lagoon also added to the fear in all the children. There was a hot band of air near the bridge, which Jonjon's older brothers and sisters kept talking about. It was thought this frightening hot air belonged to the spirits of dead persons that supposedly haunted the area.

Close to the bridge was an old house where a quiet, old woman lived. The house was partly hidden by a huge mango tree. Jonjon, his two little sisters and little brother could not see everything that was happening near to the house, but at times there would be a huge fire burning in the yard. At nights, Neeta would relate to all the children who gathered at her house all her umpteen *jumbie* (ghost) stories scaring the daylights out of the children before they left her premises. Intensifying the "horror" of the hot air around the bridge, she kept reminding Jonjon and his younger siblings that the old woman who lived in the old house near to the bridge could be a *soucouyant*, a shape-shifting Caribbean folklore character who appears as a reclusive old woman by day. By night, she strips off her wrinkled skin and puts it in a wooden mortar. In her true form as a fireball, she flies across the dark sky in search of a victim from whom she will suck blood. Neeta said that the only way that one could get rid of a soucouyant was to sprinkle salt near to one's front door. The soucouyant cannot get past the door unless all the salt grains are counted. If sunrise catches her counting the salt she would incinerate herself and vanish forever. Neeta swore that this alleged soucouyant sucked her several times as evidenced by the blue-black marks she had all over her body.

All of this talk was frightening to everyone especially when Jonjon had to cross the bridge at nights with his two little sisters and his little brother. Sometimes someone in the group would shout phrases such as "soucouyant behind yuh," or "look ah duenne in di bush," and what ensued was a mad rush to cross the bridge at a hundred miles per hour; yes, faster than Olympic 100-meter, gold medalist Usain Bolt. Breathlessly Jonjon and his siblings would reach the other side and would start laughing at their stupidity. Indeed Jonjon sensed the hot air coming from the bridge. Years later Jonjon discovered that it could have been the bacterial activity under the bridge that gave rise to hot air in that particular vicinity.

Neeta was a great and captivating storyteller; yes, she knew how to make one's eyes "google" with amazement mingled with a good dose of fright. The modulation and tone of her voice was hypnotic. Despite the fact that everyone knew that they would be scared stiff after the story, the children always wanted to hear a *jumbie* story; a ghost story from her. In those days there wasn't any television, computers, I-pads, tablets, or cell phones to keep the children occupied. Invariably, all the children craved a story, and Neeta always had a good one to keep their ears cocked. Everyone's special place to hear the story was on the back steps of Neeta's house. On most occasions Jonjon sat right next to her. The darkened steps had no light except for a flashlight in case someone wanted to use the toilet. The use of the toilet was rare since all the listeners were too scared at times to even move. Unless someone had somebody to accompany him to the toilet the person had to hold his bladder. One night, Neeta related one of her best stories; the story was about the frightful "Manicou Jumbie."

Most people in Trinidad and Tobago know what a manicou is, but for those who do not know, here is a brief description. Probably a Taino (Carib/Arawak) derivative, the term *manicou* is the name assigned to the opossum found in Trinidad. For the most part, the manicou eats fruits such as mango, ripe bananas, and pommerac, but would also act as a kind of scavenger in the clean-up of other dead animals and faecal matter. According to legend, the manicou has the unique habit of biting into things with the attendant refusal to release its viselike grip. Probably used as a defense mechanism, the animal also emits a putrid stench when provoked. Known also as *le puant* (French—The Stinker), the manicou is a marsupial, which means that it carries its young in a pocket or pouch and sometimes on its back. In most parts of Trinidad people eat the manicou and consider the flesh a delicacy.

Figure 9. A chulha or fireside. (Photograph by author, 2015)

People in the rural areas hunt manicou at nights. If there is a pommerac tree laden with ripe fruit there is sure to be a manicou or two in the boughs. To catch a manicou, a hunter must be a good shot or be very skillful with a sharp lance attached to a long bamboo pole to *juk* (stab) the manicou and remove it from its perch. "Manicou dogs" (dogs kept for hunting the manicou) are also kept to assist in the hunt. Good manicou dogs will bark at the faintest smell of a manicou. Catching the manicou is one thing; cleaning the rat-like beast is another worrisome task. The first step in the cleaning process is to singe the hair from off the animal over a good flame in a coalpot or *chulha* (Figure 9). With the fur removed, the animal looks whitish-cream in color. Then the manicou is scraped, washed, and then gutted. However, one should not forget to remove the "stinky" glands (hunters call these glands the *mist*) or else the whole carcass will be of no use for human consumption because of the stench.

The story is told that around midnight, Neeta, her sister, her little brother, her father and their two *manicou dogs* were walking back home after visiting a friend somewhere in Warden Road. Warden Road is in James Smart, the little village east of Sangre Chiquito. Houses were few on Warden Road. Cocoa and coffee plantations with huge immortelle trees lined both sides of the road. Neeta was born on Warden Road, a place where cocoa estate culture existed. In those days, Warden Road did not have an electricity supply or street lamps.

In the light of the full moon, that particular night was as bright as day. Suddenly on a little knoll in the road a manicou appeared silhouetted against the moon. They could not understand where the beast came from or why it wanted to walk in front of them. The little manicou kept a reasonable distance and wagged its tail at intervals. Sometimes it looked back and seemingly smiled at the humans while it walked. The dogs, with their tails stuck between their legs, whined incessantly. With no intention whatever to attack this manicou, the frightened dogs stayed behind and just kept on whining. Right in front of their eyes the manicou seemed to be growing bigger and bigger. Neeta said that "dey pores raise" and they reasoned that this was no ordinary manicou.

Neeta's father was a man who knew certain kinds of *prayers* and he began to mumble one of his special prayers. Suddenly the manicou disappeared into the night with an eerie horrible laugh.

Indeed, this was a *jumbie* manicou. Neeta said that this kind of thing was a normal occurrence on Warden Road. In fact, such jumbie stories were shared everywhere amongst people involved in cocoa estate culture. Many of these stories were told to pass the time on late evenings after work. This story sounded so surreal. Could it be true? How does a person explain or interpret such a story? There were too many questions in Jonjon's little brain. Unfortunately, there were no answers.

Neeta also informed that there are manicou that hunters could never catch. When they go to hunt for manicou, some hunters are very careful about the manicou that they go after. They feel that there are manicou that are not real manicou. Neeta told Jonjon that some hunters use a lot of special prayers before they go to hunt for manicou. To Jonjon, hunting manicou seemed to be a frightful experience. The folklore he heard gave him the idea that there are some phantom manicou around; jumbie manicou are everywhere in Trinidad. Some hunters after shooting or *juking dong* the manicou down from the tree will look all over under the tree and not find the beast.

Neeta cautioned that the jumbie manicou could be found anywhere, even on Oropouche Road, and cautioned the children that they should be on the lookout for them while walking home. Such stories made Jonjon and his younger siblings stick close together when they walked on their way home at nights. On most times, no one uttered a single word. Frightened and quaking in their shoes, they listened for strange sounds and kept their eyes peeled on the road home. To them, any sound could be the sound of a jumbie. Arriving home on Adventist Street was always a great relief.

As he grew, he listened to a variety of jumbie stories that involved some aspect of Oropouche Road. Neeta also told quite a few other stories including the fictional folkloric characters that took root on the Trinidadian landscape. It is possible that West African slaves brought many of these stories to Trinidad and the Caribbean in general. Moreover, many of these stories with their

French labels, for example, *Papa Bois, Duenne, Ligahu* (Loup Garou), *La Diablesse, Gumbogleezay, Mama Dlo* (Mama L'eau), and the fearsome *Soucouyant* probably arrived with their African names, but on contact with the French planters in Trinidad, the Africans adopted new tags and descriptions.

The Ghanaian name for the "Father of the forest" is *Sasabonsam*. This is probably Papa Bois in Trinidadian folklore. Papa Bois is also known as *Maître bois* (Master of the woods) or *Daddy Bouchon*. He is said to be married to *Mama Dlo* (Mama D'leau—Mother of the Waters). Considered to be the "Father of the forest," Papa Bois protects the animals in the forest. Legend has it that Papa Bois allows hunters to capture exactly one hundred animals in the forest for food. If the hunter is greedy and kills more animals, Papa Bois captures the hunter and holds him in the forest for the rest of his life where no one can find him. Worse yet, if that hunter should tread or step on "*lost vine*," that person would be lost forever in the forest. Don't try searching. That person will never be found. The name of this vine speaks for itself. Sometimes, Papa Bois would transform the hunter into another beast or bird and sadly, no one would ever see him again.

Always wearing a wide-brimmed straw hat that almost covers the face, the Duenne is said to be embodiment of a baby who died before being baptized. Duennes are terrible little creatures that tend to hang out around homes where little children live and make a whooping sound to lure them into the forest. The Duenne's feet are back to front. The heel is in the front so it becomes difficult to tell the direction a Duenne has taken. According to the stories Jonjon heard, it is known that if a Duenne captures a child, this child will be lost forever.

Mama Dlo, a huge, long snake with the head of a woman, is considered to be the protector of the rivers. She severely punishes people who disturb the flow, pollute, and disrespect the rivers of the land. Her name is Ghana is "Mamie Water." The La Diablesse, on the other hand is a very dangerous jumbie woman who has a human foot and one cow hoof. She is very pretty and whispers to her suitors many alluring words in a siren-like manner. Caught in her trap, she lures her suitors away and kills them. Some people say that La Diablesse disappears with a horrid and eerie laugh when they strike a match to light up a cigarette. It is believed that she dislikes tobacco smoke. Such were the stories, myths, and legends the children learnt from Neeta.

All of the children were conditioned at an early age to "respect" people, everyone with whom they came in contact with, because as Neeta said, there were good people and "jumbie people" who lived on Oropouche Road. One had no way of telling the "jumbie people" from the good people. It was a path the children had to choose; respect one's elders, trust no one, and just go about one's business. Prove all things and hold fast to that which is good.

Many adults secretly spoke about the terrible *Greenface Man.* They said he lived a solitary life in a small dark concrete house, a hovel on Peetams Trace. Peetams Trace was a little backroad offset from the main Oropouche Road causeway. His front door would only be half-opened, and no one ever saw his windows ajar. His attire was a pair of dirty looking khaki pants and long-sleeved khaki shirt. The way he wore his frazzled and weather-beaten felt hat indicated that he did not want people to look him in the eye. Maybe it was just his gait that sold him off as a threat to the community.

The worst thing about this man was the fact that he seemed to have no job, no place of work, and walked about just dragging a pair of busted up rubber slippers. He was thought to be the Greenface Man whom all women feared. People on Oropouche Road surmised that he had the power to get into people's houses through a keyhole to interfere with the woman of the house, and that interference was serious. Some referred to him as a *gumbogleezay* man. According to the grapevine, the gumbogleezay man is a person who shifts his shape so that he can pass through a keyhole to gain entry into someone's home. He is thought to use substances, for example, chloroform and other evil concoctions which cause people to fall into deep sleep in order for him to orchestrate his baleful activities. Just hearing about him scared the daylights out of people living on Oropouche Road.

Understanding and/or interpreting the spiritual trappings of life on Oropouche Road was as bizarre as it gets. In those days, there was something definitely frightful about Oropouche Road. Nevertheless, there were some real events that Jonjon liked as a child. Going up to the *El Reposo* farm, the government's agricultural demonstration farm, was one of his favorite pastimes. On Sundays, his elder sisters and brothers used to take him for walks to the government's demonstration farm. He developed a love for the farm. On the farm there were goats, pigs, chickens, rabbits, ducks, cows, cocoa trees, and pommerac trees.

Although the pigpens were smelly, he adored the tiny pink piglets. Their little shrill oinking sounds were also quite fascinating to him. There were also some big "ram" goats on the station--and what a putrid smell they emitted. The tall pommerac trees growing on the eastern side of the farm served as a windbreak for the cocoa trees in the demonstration plots. Jonjon's eldest brother and his friends would climb the laden trees and shower on Jonjon and his sisters the big red to purple colored fruit; the deeper the purple color of the fruit, the sweeter it tasted.

Despite the pleasant feelings engendered by visiting the farm, there were other mysterious trappings on El Reposo Road that frightened the daylights out of some of the residents on Oropouche Road and surrounding districts. As Jonjon mentioned before, street lighting was absent from the area and many activities occurred under the cover of thick darkness. The story is told that many times at midnight a full-sized wooden coffin tied with a heavy rope appeared in the middle of Oropouche Road near to the farm. People were afraid of this coffin. Later it was discovered that the coffin was used to convey ripe cocoa pods from one cocoa plantation to another. In other words, people were stealing each other's cocoa, and what better means of transport could there be but a coffin; an object of fear for many people in Trinidad.

Apart from the Gumbogleezay or "Greenface Man", Jumbie Manicou, Duenne, Ligahu, la Diablesse, Papa Bois, Soucouyant, and of course the "coffin in the road," the frightful *Banana flying ghost* was always present on the roadside. On moonlit nights there were times when an individual would swear by all heaven that he or she sighted a ghost or witnessed a spirit on a certain spot on Oropouche Road, only to realize the following day that it was just a dew-soaked, dry banana leaf blowing in the wind. The silvery looking glistening dew brought a certain kind of life to the leaf that gave to it a ghostly appearance, especially when the wind was blowing.

With regard to our belief system and our interpretation of things and activities in a system, there is a statement that we all know in Trinidad; some food for thought: "The more you watch is the less you see." This adage to some extent conveys a similarity to Anais Nin's statement: "We don't see things as they are; we see them as we are." In terms of how we all see and interpret things, Neeta had one goal, in mind. She saw money and the accumulation of wealth as her goal, her true purpose in life. Moreover, she would stop at nothing to extract from anyone, anything that she saw that would enlarge her savings, no matter how the other person felt. Neeta was not into any concept of compassion or empathy; not letting one penny slip from her grasp. She was hell-bent on making money. Using and manipulating people to create wealth was an art she developed with precision. Jonjon wondered whether some form of childhood deprivation orchestrated her attitude to the world, creating a stingy, parsimonious, avariciousness that was altogether mind-boggling for him. Indeed, Neeta's miserliness was unsurpassed in the village.

CHAPTER THREE

"Nothing is enough to the man
for whom enough is too little." (Epicurus)

"If I could get just one more egg…"

IN THEIR DISCUSSION about Neeta, many people familiar with her would declare that she was stingy, avaricious, tight-fisted, and *cheap*; cheap, in the sense that she would not spend one black cent to see the world spin. Jonjon has no reasons why she *wore* that label. What he knows is that when it comes to money, she was not a giving person; she hoarded every penny! Nevertheless, if you were hungry she would at times offer you some morsel; a piece of *sada* roti, a few *Crix* biscuits with salted butter, or a plate of rice, dhal, a piece of chicken or sliver of beef, and a tiny piece of the five-year-old, cured, black mango *amchar*. Although quite stingy, she was very hospitable and really quick to offer food. There were two or three large glass candy bottles of amchar, but you could only get one little bite of the stuff, no more. Neeta always welcomed everyone and her loquaciousness provided a noticeably calming effect on her "subjects."

After eating however, Neeta sought to extract every ounce of energy from her guests who could not leave without the accomplishment of some task for her; the calorific value of every last grain of rice, every crumb given must be *repaid* with some form of laborious work. There was always something that she wanted the guest to do for her--pure work. Some area of the yard needed to be cleaned up or weeded, some patch of grass needed to be cut, a floor must be swept and mopped, some concrete step or moss covered concrete balusters needed to be scrubbed. Neeta always had something to do! And she waited like a vulture. If one were unfamiliar about how to do a certain task, Neeta would ridicule him with the statement: "Yuh too *couyenard*," or "*couyon*," which meant that the person was stupid or *dotish*. Nevertheless, if Neeta saw that Jonjon was annoyed about calling him stupid, she was quick to counter with, "Doh mind dat *mon chere*...ah jus making joke with yuh *doo-doo*." As far as Jonjon could remember, Neeta wanted everything free, and if someone was there to be used, she would use him to the max. Neeta was extremely opportunistic. If she had to give anything to anyone Neeta would rather steal from someone else's property and then present the stolen item as a gift. Neeta was a master at enticing and sweet-talking people. She always wanted somebody to do something for her without offering any payment. Her style of cajoling was laced with persistent *mamagism*. Her use of the word mon chere was applied ad lib, probably the most frequent word that came from her lips.

Although he loved Neeta as his godmother, as a child, Jonjon saw the misnomers; the incongruities of this woman. By her actions she contradicted everything he was taught at home, at school, and at church. Like *Solomon Grundy*, he stood in his shoes and sometimes wondered about what made her into what she was. How did Neeta come to be so covetous; so greedy, so money hungry? Why did she see money as the only solution to her problems? Jonjon wanted so much to tell her that she was stealing and doing wrong, but the society and era in which he grew did not allow the young to correct or reprimand the elders. Children were told to respect their elders, no matter what, and speak only when they were spoken to. Most times, children could not even ask questions.

Stealing other people's agricultural produce was second nature to Neeta. It was as though everybody's property, in her eyes, was there for the taking. Whether it was grapefruit or cocoa pods, Neeta would always say during an act of stealing, "Dey eh go miss dat." It is extremely difficult for Jonjon to bring to the fore all the atrocities she committed in his presence in broad daylight. Jonjon's fears and worries about her plagued his mind, not knowing in whom he should confide. He did not carry any negative report about Neeta to his mother for fear that he would not be able to visit Neeta again. He found himself between a hard place and a rock. For Jonjon, visiting his godmother was a sort of escape from home and the din of eight siblings who were fighting for their own space in a tiny house. Sometimes the grass is not always greener on the other side. Jonjon guessed that if the police had come to arrest Neeta for praedial larceny he would have been asked quite a few questions about her. Maybe he would have had to join her in the *Black Maria*, the police vehicle that transports prisoners. Jonjon was instructed at home, school, and at church to be true, honest, just, and good, and to leave people's property alone. It was apparent that Neeta wanted everything for nothing, even by stealing. Jonjon wondered if Neeta had a conscience. She stole without even thinking. She wanted the world quickly, and despite their need, she never gave a cent to anybody or any church. No beggar could get a cent from Neeta. She once said: "Ah have tuh wuk too hard fuh mih money just tuh gih people." Apparently Neeta was saving up some hard cash to invest in a piece of cocoa land, loosely referred to as "cocoa estate." Unbeknownst to Jonjon she indeed acquired a mixed plantation consisting of cocoa, coffee, citrus fruit, bananas, and other miscellaneous fruit crops.

Prior to the purchase of the cocoa estate situated at Kowlessur Road, Neeta lived in a very comfortable residence located on Oropouche Road, Sangre Grande. Although he never saw her sewing clothes for anyone on her sewing machine, Jonjon learnt that Neeta used to be a good seamstress. Her house was just about half of a mile from the Eastern Main Road. The two-bedroom, two-storey concrete house was a nice looking dwelling for its time. Several citrus fruit trees surrounded the house. To the front on the right side there was a huge grapefruit tree that produced large white marsh grapefruit in profusion. Along the left side there were four king orange trees. These trees did not produce so bountifully, but whatever they bore was sweet and delicious. To the back behind the kitchen, on the left side, were two Valencia orange trees that produced abundantly. Valencia oranges develop their sweetness during the dry season, around March to April. Neeta made it clear to all of the children that they should not pick any of the fruits in her yard for the bizarre reason that Quero had counted all the oranges on all the trees. She cautioned that Quero would be angry if he found out that some of the oranges were missing. Neeta could not fool Jonjon with her fabrications. To Jonjon this was such a big, fat, filthy lie. Jonjon knew that Neeta was stingy and he was well aware that everybody knew that too. Quero was just as bad; not a giving person at all. Sometimes, Jonjon would clean out and wash his car and Quero would not even offer him a twenty-five cent piece for his work. From his right pocket, he would at times reveal a wad of dollars in front of Neeta. Jonjon could see in her eyes that she really envied the amount of money that Quero made every day from driving his Ford Zephyr taxi. O how Neeta wanted to get her hands on some of that money.

As one of the followers of *Islam*, Quero was the son of an *imam* who resided in the village of Fishing Pond. With a serious aversion for pork and pork products, there was always a little contention in the house between Neeta and Quero. Islam forbids the eating of pork. Neeta loved salted pigtail and ham. Neeta was a professed Catholic with leanings in the practice of Obeah; different lifestyle. Quero became extremely infuriated one day when he discovered that someone had purchased salted pig tail and used his lunch bag as a means of conveyance. Because of this, he cursed Neeta in patois intermingled with other expletives in "English" for over an hour. The extremely heated exchanges between Quero and Neeta were quite furious, but there was one good thing, their arguments never came to blows. Nevertheless, Neeta tried her utmost to please her husband by providing hot meals for him every day. Hot sada roti with some form of *talkaree* accompanied with homemade coffee or *Red Rose* green tea, was Quero's constant breakfast. Any leftover roti would certainly be consumed when he came home for lunch or dinner. Quero could not do without roti.

During the week, lunch or dinner consisted of white rice, *dhal*, *bhagi*, curried chicken or stewed beef, and cucumber salad. Dhal was made with yellow split peas boiled up with garlic, *geera* (cumin), turmeric powder, salt and a tad of hot pepper. After boiling, Neeta would *gotay* the contents of the pot with the use of a *dhalgotni* to bring the dhal to its right consistency. She was a master at making good dhal. Stewed beef clod was more common at meals because Quero almost got the beef free of charge. Quero raised beagle hounds for hunting game such as agouti and deer. These hounds consumed meat dust boiled up with *dog rice*. His former work colleagues at the supermarket where he once was an employee would stash a few pounds of beef clod in between the meat dust that fell from the saw. Quero paid a few cents for the cuts of beef clod hidden in between the meat dust. It is possible that he paid the meat cutter a little tip for the "extra" meat. Many times Jonjon would see Quero "playing" with the food with his right hand, mixing the bhagi, dhal, and rice into an unpalatable looking mass. He would sometimes say to Jonjon, "Dat is wuh we call *sannay*. Yuh must learn how tuh sannay...and this is the way yuh does eat with yuh hand," as he formed and pushed a small white, green, and yellow ball of food into his mouth with his thumb. Never did he use his left hand to sannay. He was a Muslim and it is well-known that the left hand is used only for sanitary purposes in cleaning one's self. It would seem that the *taria* had no need of washing when Quero was done. Every drop of dhal, every spot of bhagi, and every grain of rice was wiped clean with his right index finger. After the instant "plate washing" he would quip, "Yuh see, yuh see, yuh doh have tuh wash dat again...watch it, it clean like ah bird's ass." Despite her dutifulness to Quero, Neeta did not receive the best treatment from him. Quero was loud, rough, crass, and uncouth.

Although Neeta was legally married to Quero, Jonjon gathered from certain nuances that she was not well accepted by Quero's family. Jonjon felt the tension when she was around Quero's sisters. Quero's sisters were very uppity. They acted as though they were more fortunate than Neeta. As the custom was, Neeta would visit Quero's family on *Eid-ul-Fitr*, the day when the crescent moon was sighted at the end of Ramadan. Ramadan or *Sawm* is one of the pillars of Islam, the month designated for fasting among Islamic believers.

Awkward and uncomfortable are the best words to describe how Neeta felt among Quero's family. Jonjon was but a child and could not really understand the inter-family dynamics, the arguments, and the religious posturing. During this celebratory gathering there was always much commotion, heated discussions, and never-ending arguments among the men about what is right, who is right, and who is wrong. Arguing about religion lends itself to this kind of behavior. Neeta was a type of Cinderella. In the eyes of her mother-in-law and her sisters-in-law, the way they looked at her was enough for Jonjon to conclude that Neeta was not really accepted. Quero's father seldom spoke to Neeta. Neeta told Jonjon that she felt *genneh* when she was around them. Jonjon himself felt out-of-place. Quite noticeable was the fact that Neeta always sat downstairs even if she was eating a meal and she never sat with Quero's family upstairs at their table.

On Sundays, Neeta engaged herself in the cooking of "Sunday lunch." By Trinidadian cultural standards, Sunday lunch is a special meal. *Macaroni pie*, rice, stewed red beans, and *callaloo*, were cooked for a typical Sunday lunch. Sometimes blue crab and/ or salted pork snout or salted beef were added to the callaloo. Stewed or curried chicken, beef, or duck, slices of ripe plantain, sweet potato, dasheen, yam, or other ground provisions, fresh, crisp watercress, and on most times, potato salad with small cubes of boiled beetroot were also served as part of the fare.

On some Sundays, Neeta would make *dhalpourri* roti. Neeta made the best tasting dhalpourri. The ball of stuffed flour or *loi* is rolled flat and thin with a *belna*, or rolling pin on a *chawki*, a round board made for rolling out roti. Roasting on the *tawah*, and flipped a couple times with a *dabla*, the piping hot dhalpourri smelled and tasted so good when eaten with curried chicken or curried goat. As it came hot off the tawah, Quero would shake out the ground dhal from inside the roti into the meat sauce and begin to *bowray*. Despite the fact that there are some people who use "knife and fork" to consume roti, typically, cutlery is not used in the eating of dhalpourri. The hand and fingers are better suited for roti eating activity.

Figure 10. In this photograph, the *tawah* is standing to the back, the *chawki* is lying to the front, and on top the chawki is the *dabla* to the left, the *belna* to the right and the *dhalgotni* in the middle. (Photograph by author, 2018).

Always more tired than everyone else, Quero would come home and just sit there waiting to be served. Neeta brought everything to him. If she forgot anything for the table, for example, amchar or pepper sauce, he would promptly say, "*Gyul* (girl) bring di pepper for mih nah, and while yuh dey, bring ah big glass ah cold water fuh mih." Neeta never refused to do anything for Quero. She was always on her feet while Quero was around. Was it duty? Was it love? Was it fear? Jonjon could not determine what really held the two together. They were such opposites. In this case, it was proven that opposites do attract.

On the right side of the house, just outside the bedroom where Neeta slept stood two tall and thin avocado trees. During the bearing season, the two trees became heavily laden with fruit, but there was one problem. Apparently some owls loved the position of these trees and found a home in their branches. Every night the owls began their eerie hooting and screeching just outside Neeta's bedroom. As everyone knew, Neeta was quite superstitious. She believed that these owls were bearers of bad tidings. To her the presence of owls was an omen that someone would be facing the "grim reaper" very soon. In fact, it is well known that many Trinidadians prefer not to have owls around their premises because they feel that owls carry death on their wings. She had to somehow get rid of these pesky owls. One night in anger Neeta reached for a full *posey* (night pot) of stale urine from under her bed. Quietly she opened the window, and in seconds, the owls acquired a good bath of stale piss while she yelled repeatedly, as though crazed, "Take dat in allyuh mudder so-and-so!" She probably woke up the neighborhood. The hapless owls never returned.

With all the "owl chasing," noise, disgust and commotion, Quero rose up in anger from his sleep, and, as his custom was, started "cussing" out Neeta because of the disturbance. "Yuh is ah so-and-so nuisance! Ah fed up ah yuh so-and-so harassment! Ah man eh have ah chance with yuh. O gawd man!" he yelled. Neeta retorted: "Why yuh eh shut yuh so-and-so stinking mouth...yuh mudder so-and so!" In the adjacent room Jonjon could not contain his quiet laughter. He had to actually bury his face in his *bois flot*-filled pillow for fear that they might hear him. Just hearing her "cussing" out the owls was enough. When the bacchanal started with Quero it was the icing on the cake; so amusing. There was a full half-hour exchange of illicit words, invectives, definitions and descriptions between the two. Suddenly there was respite. In the morning Quero greeted her by stating, "yuh too so-and-so stupid!" By the way, the stale urine was kept under her bed for one reason, to ward off the soucouyants that she believed sucked her repeatedly. It is possible that the urine generated a level of ammonia that did the trick to keep soucouyants at bay; so she thought. Neeta was also wary of the *shwete,* or "The Bird of Death." This bird would sometimes fly over the house uttering a shrill cry that sounded like "shwete." Whenever the bird passed, Neeta would rise up and angrily curse this bird with such vitriol, your ears would hurt. Suspicion and superstition always got the better of Neeta, but Jonjon could not be bothered by her antics.

After the acquisition of her cocoa estate in Sangre Chiquito, Neeta began traveling with Quero her taxi-driver husband from her place of abode on Oropouche Road to Kowlessur Road. Early every morning they would pack up Quero's taxi car with all things necessary for a day's work in the cocoa field. On her return every night Neeta would put everything she needed for the day's work in "walk way" as she would always say. The way she pronounced "walk way" sounded as though she was saying "wuk way." In any case, the word "wuk" in Trinidadian dialect means "work," so to Jonjon, it did not make a difference; wuk or walk, it amounted to the same hard work he had to do on the plantation. He never asked her what the correct word was. Putting things in "walk way" or "wuk way" meant that she did not want to forget one iota that she needed for the day ahead up in Kowlessur Road. Leaving her fancy divan set of chairs in her living room, dining suite, fancy dishes, refrigerator, pipe-borne potable water supply, electricity, shower bath, spring-filled bed, and flushing toilet, Neeta decided to take up "permanent" residence in her little one bedroom makeshift house on Kowlessur Road. In the beginning she stayed all week and came back to Oropouche Road on weekends.

Neeta was obsessed. She was totally obsessed with the idea of having plenty money, and certainly did not have enough of it. In view of this fact of not having enough money, Neeta constantly raided Quero's pockets when he fell asleep. Although Quero would be stinking mad if he found out about her monetary acquisitions from his taxi driving takings, to her, taking ten or 20 dollars was not wrong; she was bold and *brass-faced*. She realized that her trade as a seamstress was not bringing in the kind of fortune she wanted to amass. Some people owed her for years and she knew that there was no way of retrieving the money from the people who owed her for sewing their clothes. Quero's pocket made up the deficit.

Apart from the cocoa estate that she now owned, Neeta raised chickens (common fowls/yard fowls), ducks, and turkeys. At the back of the house on the adjoining lot there was a fowl run that measured about 20 feet wide by 40 feet long. Chickens, ducks, and turkeys were enclosed together in the awful smelling chicken run. Sometimes the turkeys were allowed to run free in the backyard. Dragging his wing feathers and strutting about with his pomp and pride, "puf, puf, puf," the tom would gobble loudly while the hens hung around him with their "complaining" sounds. As a child, Jonjon was afraid of the tom turkey and kept his distance from the huge bird. Neeta told him that the hens constantly complained to the tom about their lack of shoes by the sounds they made while foraging, "bare feet, bare feet, bare feet," and the tom would answer with a gobbling gruff reply, "Whe di hell ah go get money tuh buy shoes?" This explanation about turkey talk was quite interesting and amusing to Jonjon.

As he grew older, Jonjon came to understand that Neeta raised poultry as a means of making money. She sold ducks, turkeys, common fowls, and common fowl eggs. Neeta sold most of her eggs to the shopkeeper who resided at the corner of Oropouche Road and Eastern Main Road. As far as Jonjon knows, everyone preferred common fowl eggs. There is this claim in Trinidad that the yolks of common fowl eggs are much brighter in color and more nutritious, but most of all, they taste better. Depending on the number of laying hens, Neeta could only muster one dozen at a time to take to the shopkeeper for a paltry sixty cents per dozen. Jonjon observed that on a certain day, the most bizarre thing happened right in front of his eyes. Neeta sat on the back step of her house looking quite depressed, maybe more frustrated. In the egg tray, she had eleven eggs and she desperately needed one more to make a dozen. That evening, she waited and waited for another hen to lay, while mumbling, "If I could only get just one more egg ah could make ah lil change dis evening." Her chickens were running around, clucking and scratching about the run but still no egg. Neeta became impatient. The next thing Jonjon saw was Neeta in the act of actually manipulating the underside of a hen to see if an egg would soon be laid. Neeta actually counted the eggs in the belly of the fowls!

As mentioned before, Neeta was superstitious. Jonjon remembers quite well when two of Quero's young beagle hounds apparently lost their appetite. To reduce the lassitude of the pups, Neeta applied *Blue* all over the dogs to ward off what she referred to as *maljo* (mal yeux) or the evil eye. She claimed that the dogs went straying at a neighbor's house and somebody "bawled" on the dogs, or complimented with an envious eye and gave them *najaar*. Neeta told Jonjon that the rubbing of the blue stuff used in laundering clothes would get rid of the maljo and the dogs would be okay. Later down in life, Jonjon was surprised to learn that there are many, many people in Trinidad and throughout the Caribbean region in general who believe in maljo, obeah, and the whole issue surrounding najaar. To prevent maljo, there are people who would impale on a stick a blue bottle on their property, especially in their vegetable gardens to ward off the evil eye while others would tie or pin a tiny blue bag on their children's clothing to provide the same "protection."

In light of Neeta's beliefs, she did not altogether reject biblical scriptures or the religion to which she belonged. Nevertheless, she was very much interested in what Trinidadians refer to as "bad books" or "high science" books. In her desire to obtain such literature, Neeta found an address and asked Jonjon to write a letter for her asking for a list of the books. In a couple of weeks Neeta received a reply. The list was long. One night while Quero was asleep, she requested that Jonjon read out the entire list of books for her. To Jonjon, it was frightening just to read the titles of the books, far more to read such books. After reading the title list for her, Jonjon never heard another word from Neeta. Her neighbors cautioned Jonjon to be careful with Neeta because she began to indulge in reading "bad books." What was Neeta's real interest in such books? It could be that she thought such literature provided the means to do things to people that would keep them in subjection to her beck and call. Whether this was true or not, Jonjon felt that she had a kind of power, a certain degree of control over a certain person he knew only as Saga.

Standing well over six feet tall, Saga was a strong, dark-skinned, muscular man. His thick lips were quite pronounced while his receding hair gave occasion to what appeared to be a bigger forehead. Jonjon estimated that Saga was around 40 years old. Never did Jonjon see him bareheaded while riding his bicycle; he always wore a ball cap. As he rode speedily in and around Sangre Grande on his Raleigh "man bike" he would laughingly shout out to Jonjon, "Rampal!" For whatever reason, Jonjon's brothers were also called Rampal. It could have been that Saga just framed a common name for Jonjon and his siblings. Saga lived with his aging mother in a little unpainted, wooden, cottage-like house complete with windows and doors fashioned with jalousies. The house, leaning to one side, was old and dusty looking, weather-worn, and blackened by the soot expelled from passing motor vehicles.

Built opposite to the Sangre Grande police station and adjacent to a vacant building lot, the house was probably used as a mini first-aid station for injured stick fighters. Stick fighting in Trinidad and Tobago emerged from the *Kalinda*, a type of dance-like martial art that came with the arrival of Africans who were sold into slavery. Special sticks are chosen from selected trees, for example, the *Poui* tree. These sticks which measure about an inch in diameter and approximately four feet long are hand-crafted with utmost care and treated with reverence. According to tradition, most sticks or *bois* are *mounted,* or in other words, "spiritually prepared" by the user or his spiritual agent.

Almost every Saturday the vacant lot became the *gayelle* for the stick fighters or bois men who came from Sangre Grande and surrounding districts including Manzanilla, Tamana, Toco, Mayaro, and possibly Biche, and Rio Claro. Old and rusty-looking corrugated galvanized steel sheets were used to cordon off the stick-fighting arena. A flat charge of maybe two to five dollars was collected as the entrance fee to see the stick fights among the challengers. The noise of the African drums and the chanting would echo throughout Sangre Grande, and people would gather.

Many individuals who did not want to pay to see the fights would find a peep hole in the fence to witness the fervor, the *gambage* of the challengers, the sweat, and the blood that gushed from open wounds on the head. As the drumming and chanting reached its crescendo, two valiant dancers, as though in a trance, would enter the ring and start marching around back and forth posturing and sizing up each other like roosters gearing up for a fight. The drumming was louder now and suddenly, the sticks violently meet each other, "clataks, clataks, clataks." The fight commenced; the gayelle was now alive. The yelling, restless, half-drunk crowd rose with screams and applause, and the bois men, to show their aggression, leapt as roosters into the air to gain more presence, more power and agility to "pelt a good bois." Pelting a good bois was an art involving channeled strength in the flick of the wrist.

Figure 11. A stickfight, at Turure Junction, Trinidad. Look at the crowd of people behind the rope barrier. There is a pile of money in a circle between the two fighters. The one who is first to "draw blood" wins all the money (Photograph by author).

In stick fighting, winning the battle entails how well an opponent *carays,* or defends himself with his stick. In many instances, there is a great deal of bloodletting when a bois man wounds his opponent. Large cuts derived from a hard piece of wood making contact with the head of the other would open into a gushing stream of blood; time to go to the *blood hole* to bleed. To the far end of the gayelle, a place called the "blood hole" was provided for men who were cut by a bois and bleeding. Bleeding at the blood hole seemed ritualistic. It was as though the cut bois men were shedding blood for some odd purpose.

Some of the wounded would be carried over to Saga's house for a little treatment and bandages, but the drumming would once more get into them. After drinking a few shots of rum, many stickmen would jump back into the ring. Although he looked like one, Jonjon could not say whether Saga was a stick fighter. Stick fighting in Sangre Grande drew very large crowds. Although illegal, people still placed bets in the gayelle for their favorite stickman. Competitions were staged with stick fighters from all over Trinidad and Tobago. What Jonjon remembers is that Joe Pringay from Sangre Grande was the best bois man that ever lived.

On many nights, especially when she needed help with bringing in the cocoa crop, Neeta would go over to Saga's house to chat with his mother, bringing with her gifts of food, green bananas and other agricultural produce. It was as though she knew his mother for a very long time. Getting Saga to work for her was Neeta's object of the visitations. She wanted his services in the field-- nothing more. Whether Saga was paid is still a question in Jonjon's mind because he never saw Neeta giving any money to him. It's possible that Saga wanted to be included in Neeta's will, or to get some lump sum of money or a piece of the cocoa plantation when Neeta retired. Who knows why he worked so hard for Neeta and also, who knows why Jonjon spent almost all his weekends there?

CHAPTER FOUR

"When you walk with fear,
you see and hear things that are not there."

"Dah who you?"

T HE FARE WAS only four cents for the bus ride from the Sangre Grande police station to the Kowlessur Road junction on Manzanilla Road. Despite the paltry sum of money for the bus fare, four cents was quite expensive for Jonjon. Nevertheless, he saved the money to take the bus on weekends. His short journey, just about five miles, was a bit unnerving for him while riding the Public Transport Service Corporation (PTSC) bus. There was a bit of trepidation for a ten-year-old boy hopping a bus on his own. If there was room, Jonjon sat in a seat mainly at the front close to the conductor, and would sometimes remind the conductor that he was stopping at the Kowlessur Road junction.

Most of the people on the bus were discreetly silent, probably too tired to speak. Some of the older folk breathed low sighs while others nodded violently and incessantly. As Jonjon stared at some of them for a few moments, he swore that their heads would certainly pop and fall off. It was apparent that all the passengers knew one another. This was *their* bus after work. When someone was not paying attention to their stop, somebody would hail out to the conductor to stop the bus. This happened frequently. It was very rare that anyone spoke with Jonjon. He had to find his way for himself. With his eyes peeled on the road and the signs nearing the Kowlessur Road junction in the dimming light, he had to be certain when to press the stop button lest he go too far up on the Manzanilla Road.

On arrival at the junction on late Saturday evenings, with the sun dipping low behind the patches of 200 foot tall bamboo and immortelle trees, he would walk a distance of three-quarters of a mile to the little make-shift wooden country house on Neeta's cocoa plantation. Along the road, unseen frogs with their chorus of "poounk kah nak, poounk kah nak...poounk, poounk, poounk" joined in unison as they continued their repetitious mating calls. Creating an irrepressible evening orchestra were the crickets with their high-pitched, shrill chirping, the intermittent calls of other animals and birds intermingling with the music of the frogs; a literal din, a pandemonium of almost deafening proportions greeted Jonjon's ear. It seemed every single frog and every single cricket wanted to be heard above each other simultaneously. The animal calls of the evening reminded him that daylight would soon disappear.

The day was dying fast and night was quickly falling. Jonjon had no choice but to hasten his footsteps on the rough asphalt surface. He could not take the chance to walk in the dark for fear of serpents that might be lurking around. The road was narrow. Barely two vehicles could pass each other on this road, but seldom did he ever see a vehicle at that hour. Without a supply of electricity, street lamps, or potable water lines, this asphalt covered road was once a *bridle* road traversed by donkeys, horses, and mules. Such draught animals were especially valuable in the days when cocoa was king.

Flanked with cocoa, citrus, stands of banana, and coffee fields on both sides, the darkening environment became creepy and frightening for Jonjon, especially when he remembered Neeta's jumbie stories about *papa bois*, the *duennes*, the *soucouyants*, and the dreaded *ligahu* (Loup Garou). There was always this fear

45

in his mind that something horrible would jump out of the bushes to grab him. The cultivations were now void of light, and even though Jonjon never saw the animal, the infamous bird he knew as the "*Dah Who You*" bird, kept repeating its questioning call. As though asking him a question as he hastily walked the long, lonely, and dreary road, the bird was relentless in voicing: "Dah who you? Dah who you? Dah who you?"

As a matter of interest, and funny as it may sound, the story is told about a Grenadian cocoa estate laborer when he first appeared on the scene. He was confronted with the same *question* with this bird calling out to him, "Dah who you? Dah who you? Dah who you?" He had no idea that the sound came from a bird; a secretive bird offering its evening call. In the twilight, almost to tears, frozen with fright while toting on his head a box of groceries, he stopped and answered the call of the *Dah who you* bird: "Is me frere Jarge (George) from Gouyave, Grenada…ah come hyah tuh look fuh wuk in di cocoa plantation and now yuh asking mih who is me? I never see more nah. Wuh yuh want from mih? Wuh troubles reach mih hyah? "O gawd, why yuh doing mih this?" The bird continued its call. He thought that someone hiding in the bush sought to do him harm. Releasing his grip from the box of groceries, he fled in terror, like a bat out of hell. On reaching the wooden barracks where he resided on the *white man* estate, he fainted and fell flat in front of his door. His poor wife had to give him some smelling salts and a drink of rainwater to revive him. What an ordeal it was for frere Jarge. Frere Jarge never heard anything like that in Grenada. Whether this narrative is true, it was Neeta who told to Jonjon this story about frere Jarge. Jonjon took Neeta's story with a "pinch of salt" because she always had some fable up her sleeve.

From the junction of Kowlessur Road there were a few small houses, for the most part five or six structures erected mainly on the right side of the road. Almost all of them were unfinished and ramshackle. After those houses there appeared a long houseless incline that changed immediately around a sharp corner to a rough downhill trot that ended into a stretch of flat cocoa lands with huge ravines flowing through them. This part of the floodplain of Kowlessur Road was known as *Lillyto Flats*, a toponym assigned to the area probably because of the name of the owner of that particular cocoa field. Under the culvert of one of the ravines there was a nest of the aestivacious (dormant during the dry season) fish known as the *chatto*. This bony-plated catfish is a delicacy for many people in Trinidad. Unlike the *cascadura*, the chatto has a flattened head, and some say it tastes just as good in a coconut curry as the cascadura; the more sophisticated and desirable cousin. In one of his descriptions about Trinidadian folklore, the Trinidadian writer Samuel Selvon cited about some lines Allister Macmillan wrote: "Those who eat the cascadura will, the native legend says, wheresoever they may wander end in Trinidad their days" How true is this statement? I cannot give any evidence of this as fact, but one of Jonjon's American friends for this reason said that he will never ever taste a cascadura. Nevertheless, Jonjon and his little brother had the time of their lives fishing for chatto in that very spot. They lifted so many of them that some of the big ones had to be kept for a period of time swimming around in a concrete barrel at Neeta's.

For all the time Jonjon spent in Kowlessur Road, no one in the area knew that fishing spot. It was a wonderful discovery! Jonjon and his little brother pulled out many nice chatto specimens from that ravine. It was just amazing how many there were under the culvert, and they were hungry. Despite the feeding frenzy, Jonjon and his brother left some for another day. Then someone opened their mouth and disclosed the location. While traveling in Quero's car, Jonjon saw a shopkeeper from off the Manzanilla Road literally taking every last fish from his favorite fishing hole. Jonjon was saddened at this fact but there was little that he could have done. Not one chatto was left; illustrative of "the tragedy of the commons," a situation where greedy people harvest more than they need. The "common man" does not leave any for another day. Because he has no idea of conservation or preservation, he takes all today.

Figure 12. It's still there, the bamboo patch
on the hill in front of Mimae and Flemo's house.
(Photograph by author, 2014)

Escaping the darkened dread of the Lillyto Flats and the fearful call of the "Dah who you" bird, Jonjon was happy to be in a little more light as the sun slipped slowly behind the tall bamboo patch (Figure 12) around the corner where Mimae and her husband Flemo lived. Although the "Wuk Well" bird joined in the chorus with its call, "Yuh wuk, yuh wuk well" at the close of the day, this part of Jonjon's walk was less fearful, more joyous, and lighthearted; a relief since Neeta's house was just about 500 to 600 paces away. On the right side of the road, the topography changed once more. The landscape rolled into hills and dales, revealing a tiny village with some denizens who would serve as special characters in the stories involving the Cocoa Woman.

Mimae and Flemo lived in a little bamboo and dirt wattle hut on the summit of a hill almost measuring the same elevation as Neeta's house. Because of the huge bamboo patch, the hut was hardly recognizable from the road below. No one knew whether anyone really lived on that hill, only the presence of a thin wisp of smoke that emerged from the *chulha* that faded as it rose over the tops of the bamboo patch signaled the presence of life there. Never once did Jonjon walk up the steep reddened dirt path on that hill to Flemo's house. In fact, he was told never to go there. Neeta cautioned that Flemo and Mimae were not the type of company that he should keep. Flemo was an alcoholic. The scent of booze was always on his breath. A brown colored tobacco pipe was always stuck between his drooping lips at the corner of his mouth. He lived his life for the moment, and he never cared if Sunday fell on Monday.

Mimae stuttered and also stammered. Presenting a greasy, round face, her almost toothless mouth would mumble some words in quick succession. It was always difficult to understand her erratic speech while she manipulated a half-burnt, non-filter *Anchor Special* cigarette between her discolored lips, as though she was eating, smoking, laughing, and talking at the same time.

In a calf-length, unhemmed, heavy, dirty, brown cotton dress that swung on her shoulder like a sack, Mimae walked barefooted up and down Kowlessur Road. Neeta said that Mimae had relatives living in London and they would usually send to her a couple dresses; dresses she wore down to rags. Moving swiftly from side to side, as though questioning everyone's move, Mimae's eyes had a wild focus somewhat like a crazed, trapped cat. Her gait was an untidy, stomping, aggressive march. Her calloused feet looked tough; her toes that were spread apart like a fan never looked clean or washed. It was noticeable that fissures in the thickened skin of her feet overpowered her muddied heels. Her tough curly hair was short and matted, probably not seeing a comb or brush for an extended period of time. Her greasy face offered obvious signs that Mimae was hygienically challenged; a person's olfactory lobes would go into high alert when Mimae passed by. It was obvious that she did not see the need of a bath or the maintenance of dental care. Mimae also did not care about cleansing her muddied feet.

Most people in the little village that sprung up in the recesses of Kowlessur Road avoided Mimae. Despite her unkempt attire and seemingly rough grunting responses, the residents in the little village would still hail out to her with a daily greeting; they more or less pitied Mimae's penury. Nevertheless, when harvest time for the cocoa, coffee or citrus (grapefruit) crop came around Mimae would find herself up the hill at Neeta's house in a quest for work. Throughout the year Neeta would intermittently employ Mimae to do little menial tasks and odd jobs, but during "croptime" every hand was needed. With enough labor, Mimae collected quite a few dollars for her work. Mimae never wore any protective covering on her feet. She worked in the same dress. Jonjon never saw her in any other form of attire.

Hired to help harvest the coffee crop, Mimae would pick one or two baskets of ripe coffee berries for her day's work. A basket of ripe coffee berries weighed around 50 pounds. She would be paid at the end of the day a sum of ten Trinidad and Tobago dollars per basket. Flemo would sometimes come in to help her while she worked to fill her baskets. Coffee picking is tough work which required a large sheet or *pal* constructed from several pieces of hemp or jute bags sewn together. Jonjon knew these bags as "blue seam" bags. These blue seam bags were also useful in the making of durable hammocks, one of which was hung under the shed outside Neeta's country house. Sometimes eight to ten feet in diameter, the pal would be spread and moved around under the branches of the coffee trees to collect the ripe berries. After picking the clusters on the branches there would be several leaves and twigs mixed in with the berries. Two people would then winnow the contents of the pal, remove the trash and pour the berries into a basket. Jonjon had his full share of picking coffee. The poem below titled "Coffee Picker" illustrates this sentiment.

Ripe red berries
Prettify the greenery
Dazzling cherries in the sunlight,
Pickers work from dawn till night.

Spread the pal with utter contempt!
That big brown stinking sheet of hemp
Gather, save; salvage every bean,
Rape the tree, pick it clean.

Hook the branch into a bow
Pull, bring it down low
Never mind if the friggin' thing breaks,
Anger and hate my soul overtakes.

Large black, biting ants join the feast
Fall in clusters on man and beast
Sweat; never mind what it takes,
Coffee picking has no brakes.

Scorpions and snakes in the cluster too
To bite and sting in the coffee brew
Smell the aroma of the fetid, stinking money,
For coffee pickers, pennies only.

Most of the coffee trees were of the *Robusta* variety that bore profusely. Although touted for its fine flavor, the few old stands of *Arabica* coffee trees present on the plantation did not produce much. The ripe red coffee berries attracted all kinds of arthropods inclusive of scorpions and spiders. Black biting ants would also nest in the leaves of the trees and sometimes a snake or two would fall on the shoulders of coffee pickers. The snakes were present because of the other creatures around that served as their food source. There is a food chain in every living system. Jonjon remembers Eula, one of the hired coffee pickers, who was very, very afraid of the snakes. If she saw a snake she would drop everything in her hand and run, really run far, very far away from the tree yelling "O gawd! O gawd! O gawd! Snake! Snake! Snake! Jesus! O gawd!" as she ran. Eula could not control her hysteria when she saw the little green non-poisonous snakes hanging from the coffee branches. It was so much fun to see skinny, redskin Eula traveling at light speed in the bush; literally floating through the field like a water skipper on a lake.

Eula came to work quite early, and with bulging eyes, the first thing she would say to Jonjon was, "SSSSnake! Snake! Snake!" That was her way of saying "Good morning" to Jonjon. To get to Neeta's house, Eula walked through the unpaved southern portion of Kowlessur Road that began on the Cunapo Southern Main Road or Biche Road. It meant that a person could have walked from the Kowlessur Road junction on Manzanilla Road right through to the Biche Road a little way beyond a village known as Coalmine Village (see Figure 13).

When Flemo was not helping Mimae he would be occupied in *cutlassing* cocoa trees for anyone who would employ him. Cocoa production is dependent on good management of the trees. Keeping the roots of the cocoa trees free of weeds is very important; the less competition with weeds, the better for the cocoa crop. Manual cutlassing of cocoa plantations is quite a laborious job. Cutlassing requires strength, fortitude, and a certain kind of art in wielding the *swiper* or *brushing cutlass*. In those days a man would receive a mere five cents to clear one cocoa tree of brush (tall bush). Not only was the *cutlass man* required clearing the heavy bush, he also understood that it was his chore as well to *roundeer* the root of the cocoa tree and clean off the excess moss on the trunk of the tree as far as his hands would allow. Cleaning the moss off the trunk of the tree and light pruning of all unwanted *chupons,* aids with the production of more flowers on the cocoa tree. More flowers on the *cushions* of the cocoa trees mean more pods (Figure 14).

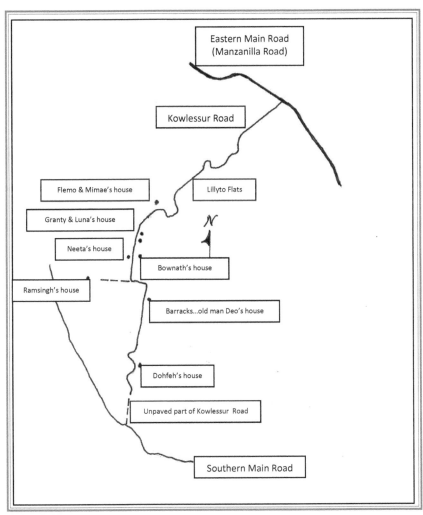

Figure 13. Sketch map of the tiny village inside Kowlessur Road (nts).

Figure 14. The cushion and flowers on a cocoa tree
(Photo credits, Leon Granger, 2015. Used with permission)

Cocoa pods develop on both the branches and trunks of cocoa trees. When pods are ripe, care must be taken to not damage the cushions or the branches when harvesting the pods. The bumps on the trunk of the tree from which the flowers emerge, or the cushions, are very important for the next year's cycle of production. A clean cut with a sharp blade or gullet through the stem of the pod is advised. Too many *chupons* or excessive vegetative growth at the base of the tree could also reduce the production of pods. So apart from actually brushcutting or cutlassing, the cutlassman or woman had to make sure that all the cocoa trees looked "clean and tidy," especially on the trunk. In those days, the speed at which some cutlassmen operated astonished Jonjon and he wondered if there was some way possible to motorize a swiper or brushing cutlass.

Many men could only realize five dollars for a day's work, having *cutlassed* 100 cocoa trees. There were others who could make ten dollars for their day's work, from cutlassing from sun up to sundown. Around the cocoa plantations in Kowlessur Road, Flemo was a famous cutlass man with enough style. With his discolored pipe lodged at the corner of his mouth he would slowly pass by with a broad grin that would suggest, "You are not better than me."

Jonjon made him out to be a kind of *sagaboy* in his day. Despite his attire, he was a man full of pride. His muddied *Wellintons* (tall rubber boots) were not perfect. One side was shorter than the next, and he did not care if they were torn up because at least he had some footwear to use. Over his shoulder he carried a *crook-stick*, his *brushing cutlass*, a dirty-looking, well-worn, plastic one gallon water bottle, and a *Nicholson* file wrapped in polythene as a means of waterproof.

A brushing cutlass is a tool constructed from a flat, sharpened 18-24-inch machete (cutlass) blade bent at an angle which is then fitted with a long wooden handle and tied together with cutlass wire or binding wire (Figure 15). As the name implies, a crook-stick is a wooden tool cut from a branch with an 80° to 90° hook on a handle almost as long as the swiper handle. The hook is about four to five inches long. This special stick, sometimes cut from a coffee tree, aids someone in the act of cutlassing or brushcutting. As Neeta would say, the crook-stick offers a *peton*, somewhat of a third "foot" for greater balance.

Assuming the person is right-handed, the crook-stick is held in the left hand as a means of control to hook and pull the brush or grass, which allows clearance for the fall of the swiper blade at the base of the bush. This synchronized action allows the brush to be cut with ease. Without the crook-stick, cutlassing will be more than a chore; a definite struggle. A good crook-stick is a treasured tool. Many cutlass men do not lend out their crook-stick or brushing cutlass; these implements are more or less personal. A brushing cutlass can be called by several names including *langmat*, *swiper*, or *boze*.

Figure 15. What a brushing cutlass or swiper looks like.
This one is right-handed. (Photo by author 2016)

Flemo worked faithfully for Neeta, but there were many instances when Flemo thought that he was being robbed. Sad to say, Flemo was probably correct in his assumption. For this reason Flemo stopped working for Neeta. Although she offered a small cup of coffee sometimes to her workers, Neeta did not really care about who worked for her. She saw the dollars. That's all. Jonjon noticed the coldness between Neeta and Flemo and guessed that Neeta was trying somehow to short pay Flemo for some cutlassing work which he had done.

With Neeta, there was always some error in checking the several hundreds of cocoa trees that Flemo cutlassed. This was Neeta's management style. She always complained about the work people did for her; always dissatisfied. The work was never good enough because she never wanted to pay. It was difficult for money to leave her hands. Although she promised Flemo a better deal by raising the price to cutlass the cocoa trees, he decided that he did not want to work for her anymore. Flemo reasoned that he could not trust Neeta. One day, Jonjon overheard him saying, "Not because ah man poor and struggling yuh go want tuh take advantage ah him. Some people feel dat yuh have tuh wuk fuh Congo jawbone." With Flemo's disappointment, Mimae also stopped working for Neeta. On Neeta's plantation there was a high turnover of workers.

In many ways, Neeta's was more of a slave driver. Flemo's and Mimae's story is only one of the instances where Neeta was involved with the people on Kowlessur Road. The Kowlessur Road interior village was small, and invariably, Neeta knew everybody. Some of them said nothing to her while others became her enemy. Flemo stopped cutlassing but Quero involuntarily took up the job because he was forced by the law to stop plying his taxi for hire. Quero's two hands were now free to do some work on Neeta's cocoa plantation.

Cutlassing the cocoa field and cleaning cocoa trees was not something that Quero really wanted to do. Driving his taxi was what he liked. He wanted to see money in his hand every day. Instant gratification was his style, but things change. Having been involved in a vehicular accident, Quero was proven wrong in the incident. With his driver's permit and taxi badge taken away, he was debarred from driving his taxi for quite a few months. His new means of conveyance was a used Raleigh bicycle he purchased from a junk store. The bike served him well. He slept at nights in the house at Oropouche Road and rode on early mornings to Kowlessur Road.

Not having his usual work, Quero had time on his hands, and with a little coaxing from Neeta he agreed to do some cutlassing. Quero knew how to do a good cutlassing job. He was excellent at it and boasted to Doon his friend that he was doing a *kamayung* job, meaning it was the best type of cutlassing work you could find. He made sure that there was no *mathias* work as some cutlassmen would do, leaving the drain edges with standing grass, not carefully cleaning the roots of the cocoa trees or leaving moss on the trunk. Quero was so proud of his work that he even invited Doon, a former cocoa estate overseer to inspect his work. Doon complimented him and declared that his work was one of the best he had seen. Quero felt elated, and bragged that he was the best cutlassman ever. Quero had two swipers, and soon enough the second swiper would be put to work.

One day, Jonjon came down into the flats in the cocoa field where Quero was working to bring him some orange juice and cold water. As Jonjon sat there on the side of a box drain he looked at the swiper just standing there. In his mind he knew that he could do cutlassing. He looked at how Quero manipulated the crookstick and the swiper in unison and then he called out to Quero, "I could do that," meaning he could use the swiper and crookstick just as Quero did. Quero motioned to him to take up the swiper and the crookstick. Jonjon was excited to begin a new task, and indeed he was very successful in proving that he could do just as Quero. Jonjon felt elated that he was now growing up to do things that adults did. He felt confident that he could cutlass at least 30 to 50 cocoa trees in one day. This type of work is what he enjoyed.

As Jonjon came closer to his godmother's house he checked the little grass path on the left for the house where Granty lived with his wife Luna. Granty's house was situated in the flat to undulating lands obliquely opposite to Flemo's hillside house. Granty lived on lands that belonged to Dado Ramoo. Dado Ramoo visited his property once or twice per week. When he arrived, the whole village knew the very moment. His bellowing voice broke the silence of the quiet little village. He made sure that everyone knew that he was around. Dado Ramoo was always happy and excited to see Granty. Granty was the overseer for Dado Ramoo's entire plantation, and made sure that everything was in order. Dado Ramoo trusted him with his property. After Granty's, there was a small *tapia* (adobe) house covered with a *carat* (palm fronds) roof. Annexed to this house was an outside kitchen and chulha. Boywah, one of Dado Ramoo's hired workers resided in this little cosy shelter.

Granty lived in the house Dado Ramoo provided. The tiny house was difficult to see from the road, but sometimes Luna, his wife would be seen quietly working among the cultivated trees that lined the grassy path. Luna was a small, short, woman with a pleasant smile, not more than five feet tall. It looked as though she was a mixture of Chinese, Spanish, and Carib. Luna wore a colorful cloth head wrap, an indicator that she could have belonged to the Spiritual Baptist faith. In between the citrus trees, Luna cultivated a variety of plants including pigeon peas, *bodi*, *seim* bean, dasheen, tomato, and some medicinal plants such as *fever grass* (lemon grass), *chandilay*, *shadon beni* (bandania), and worm bush. Also growing there were huge clumps of sugar cane. While Luna tended these plants, Granty worked for Dado Ramoo as well as several other plantation owners in the village.

As an excellent *drainerman*, Granty found labor on almost everybody's plantation. Far and wide, everyone knew that he was the best drainerman around, and his enviable skill earned him much money. Jonjon knew that he worked for both Neeta and Dohfeh. Dohfeh was the single, old cocoa proprietor who lived in a cocoa house on the one and a half mile mark on Kowlessur Road. Jonjon remembers the accuracy and neatness of the box drains Granty dug for Dohfeh in a new clonal cocoa plot during the dry season. Clonal cocoa, as the name implies, are cuttings developed for planting (rooted) that were taken from highly producing and disease resistant trees. These trees are not grown from seed. Clonal trees do not grow too tall and are easier to manage. Most of the clones are produced from cultivars known as Trinidad Selected Hybrids (TSH). These cultivars are also high producing. Cocoa farmers in those days were subsidized by the government to establish new clonal cocoa plots. Dohfeh took advantage of these subsidies and greatly improved on his cocoa production.

For his age, possibly early sixties, Granty was a fairly robust looking man, about six feet tall. Granty came to work at the "crack of dawn" or as Neeta described, "day clean." By nine o'clock, he was dripping wet from head to toe. In the hot and humid weather, his brown skin and his semi-bald head shone in the morning sun as sweat poured from his body.

Stopping for a small lunch break, Granty would sit on a piece of board and lean himself against a pillar at the back of the house as the sun slid past noon. As a rule, he would eat several pieces of boiled cassava, flour dumplings, and a few chunks of dasheen slathered in a salted codfish and tomato stew after which he gulped a few mouthfuls of rain water. He was a fast talking, highly expressive person. Jonjon could hardly figure out correctly what he was saying. His face muscles rapidly adjusted to form the French creole (patois) he spoke. English or Trinidadian dialect were seldom spoken; he preferred to keep his business between Dohfeh, Neeta, and himself. Little did he know that Jonjon was learning their "secret" code. For whatever his reason(s), Granty did not want to engage in much talk with Jonjon. It could be that Jonjon was inquisitive, asking too many questions. Nonetheless, the drains were amazingly straight and the heavy *sapate'* (clayey) soil looked as though it was polished after leveling with Granty's sharp draining spade.

On some evenings, Neeta would stroll over to Granty's home for "ah lil *blague*," and naturally some "*mauvais langue*." On such evenings, Jonjon was always happy to have a cool drink of pure sugar-cane juice extracted from freshly cut canes that grew in Granty's garden. The cane juice was extracted from squeezing the mature sweet canes between two heavy poles fitted into the notch of a large tree. Under the poles was fitted a large piece of flat hardwood shaped with a recess in the middle into which the juice flowed. The two poles which acted like a huge pair of scissors were fed the raw washed canes while Granty manipulated them to squeeze out the juice. Fresh sugar cane juice is delicious especially when ice cold.

Sometimes Granty was quite secretive when speaking with Neeta and oftentimes would walk her out of the grass track to the main road. Neeta would tell Jonjon to go walk up in front while she walked slowly behind with Granty. Jonjon was not supposed to hear what they were talking about, but he heard anyway. One evening, the words *"belle femme garçon"* left Granty's lips.

There are two sayings in Trinidadian dialect that everyone knows: "Bush have ears," and "Ants go bring news." In other words, in the first case, be careful what you say, where you say it, when you say it, how you say it, and to whom you say it because some unseen guest might be listening. In the second instance, if you did not hear it when you were alive, the ants will let you know when you are dead and buried. It could be too that Jonjon's *macometer* (A cerebral *device*, especially unique to Trinidadians that facilitates detection, retention, and repetition of other people's business) was fairly high or finely tuned. The use of the term macometer implies that Jonjon was a *maco*. Jonjon was quite intelligent for his young age.

At this point in his life he was being schooled in arithmetic, verbal ability, English composition, comprehension, and reasoning ability to sit the Common Entrance Examinations (CE). Success at the CE would afford him a place in a government high school; free high school. To say that Jonjon was minding their business would be intimating that he was *farse* or nosy, having the ability to pry into the affairs of others. Jonjon was not so inclined, but he overheard some interesting snippets in their conversation; a conversation in what seemed to be veering in the direction of seeking the assistance of an obeahman, which leads to an episode in Granty's love life that requires some special attention.

Although Granty was quite comfortable with his dutiful wife Luna, he became somewhat restless because of a younger brown-skinned pretty woman he had espied. This woman resided a little higher up in Sangre Chiquito village further up from the Kowlessur Road junction on the Manzanilla Road. Not knowing what really transpired in the conversations between Granty and Neeta, Jonjon found it weird that Granty would be asking him how to capture a pair of mountains doves. To "capture" this woman, Neeta suggested to Granty that there was an obeahman who could help him. Mister Alphonzo, otherwise known as "Papa Alfonse" was the obeahman that Neeta suggested could help Granty with his problem. Granty was desperate to win the affections of the young woman. He became enthused with the idea of seeking the help of Papa Alfonse. Without hesitation, Granty decided to meet with Papa Alfonse.

Papa Alfonse was a lean, lanky, sun-burnt individual that carried a gaunt facial expression. His facial skin was drawn tight on his bony face; he looked like a living skeleton. His jawbone looked sharp as a flint. Fixed above his straight and narrow nose was a very dark pair of lens enclosed by a bronze-colored frame which he wore all day and all night; no one saw his eyes. Sitting loosely on his head was a weather-beaten straw hat, frazzled at the brim. Looking as though handmade, the pair of well-worn, almost sole-less leather sandals that showed off his bony long toes and hardened toenails complimented his washed-out blue denim "Farmer Brown" coveralls.

A multi-colored striped shirt was the only saving grace to his attire. Papa Alfonse actually looked the part of a back-in-time hippie that remained static; frozen in time. Jonjon's had serious difficulty in understanding the circumstances about this man. Papa Alfonse's almost astute silence while sitting at the table and listening to Neeta as she spoke of Granty and his request was "deafening." Papa Alfonse did not display the trappings of an obeahman at all; definitely not what Jonjon envisaged an obeahman to look like. In fact, he looked like a longtime sagaboy. The only things missing on his person to make of him a complete sagaboy were the dried squirrel's tail stuck to the side of his straw hat, and a handkerchief hanging out of his right side back pocket.

One night, Quero drove Neeta and Jonjon to pay a visit to Papa Alfonse who lived somewhere on a little track off the Valencia Old Road. It was dark and Jonjon cannot remember exactly where the house was located. When they arrived, Neeta walked up to the rickety wooden steps of Papa Alfonse's house. His small house, fitted with jalousied windows and doors was probably about 100 years old.

Neeta knocked and the door opened. There wasn't much light in the interior but she went in anyway. About five minutes later Neeta returned to the car and invited Jonjon to come see the crystal ball in Papa Alfonse's house. She said that it was amazing for her to see parts of the world and other things in the ball that she never even heard about. Neeta tried to court Jonjon into going in but Quero said: "Doh go inside dey boi. Dat eh fuh yuh tuh see. Dem doing obeah."

Despite being a rough, arrogant *"cuss bud"* at times, Quero, in a very firm manner, told Jonjon, "Stay inside di car. Doh follow she!" Quero brought Neeta to Papa Alfonse's place but was not involved in her obeah-oriented activities; he avoided obeah as the plague. This could have been the reason why Quero was so callous and behaved the way he did with Neeta cussing her out at the drop of a hat. Having read the book "Secrets of the Spirit World," Jonjon also knew that the practice of obeah was not for him. Neeta tried to influence Jonjon in many ways. Most of all she wanted him to be comfortable with stealing, but Jonjon resisted, he was not budging from the training he adopted at home, at school, and at church; the right thing was the right thing, and a wrong thing could never become a right thing.

Neeta did not stop there. Surreptitiously she made attempts for him to become engaged with objects and events that surrounded the practice of obeah, for example, she solicited his help in writing letters to certain organizations to request lists of books that were known to harbor bad elements. These books were known as "bad books." Next she requested that he make a list and labels for vials of potions, solutions oils, objects, and powders that she believed possessed magical powers wherewith she could apply to control people. Jonjon remembers that one such vial contained the dried tough yellow epithelial tissue taken from the inside of chickens' gizzards. What did she want with this stuff? Who knows? The list of oils, potions and powders included among others "Come-back-man oil," "Money oil," "Confusion powder," "Compelling powder," "Red lavender," and Guinea pepper.

Granty decided to meet with Papa Alfonse because he was serious about winning this woman. Whatever it took, Granty was willing to go the full nine yards. Papa Alfonse requested that when he visited he should bring with him a pair of mountain doves for the ceremony. These doves are pretty smart birds and are difficult to catch but Granty persevered. In his attempts to capture a pair of these doves, he was tenacious. Night and day he contemplated what he could do to catch them. Granty set some dried corn under the branch of a tree where he saw the birds feeding. The birds came and started feeding. Keeping his distance for fear he might scare the birds, Granty nervously dropped the cocoa basket trap that hung over the bait. The basket fell, but one of the birds escaped.

With one bird in hand he went to Papa Alfonse. Papa Alfonse was not too happy with Granty and scolded him for his awkwardness. He told Granty to go catch the partner to this bird because one bird would not do. Hours turned into days, days turned into weeks, but Granty was unsuccessful in catching the other bird. The captive bird was released. Bereft and broken, Granty lost his chance for capturing the young woman. All this time, Luna kept wondering about Granty's behavior and his temporary insanity. Whether Luna found out about Granty's tryst, and his deep yearning for the young woman, no one knows. Not long after, Luna died peacefully in her sleep, and for the first time Jonjon heard the sounds of the bongo drums in that village in Kowlessur Road. The monotonous drumming, the shouting, heaving, and chanting among the mourners echoed through the village for several nights. What happened to Granty after Luna died is a mystery. Granty disappeared from the village. No one knew where he went or where he ended up.

CHAPTER FIVE

When your hand is in the lion's mouth...
pull it out easy

"Respect or slavery"

DOWN THE HILL and across the road from Neeta's house lived a cocoa plantation laborer known as Claude. His short muscular frame covered with the smoothest black skin was magnificent to behold. Because of its shine, his skin actually reflected the sunlight. Jonjon found it incomprehensible to witness the laborious toil that Claude had to contend with each day. From dawn till dusk, Claude was constantly at work. He did not have a spare moment, not even to relax in the hammock that swung under the cocoa house where he lived. Rain or shine, he was up and about, stopping sometimes only for a drink of water. On Fridays the chores increased, and there was good reason.

The profusion of sweat that poured from his brow and the wet khaki shirt presented enough evidence to illustrate his haste in completing his work. His body language took on a jittery look while he engaged himself in pruning trees and shrubs, cutlassing and meticulously edging the country house lawn, cobwebbing and sweeping the verandah, and scrubbing the mud from off the concrete floor. Claude made sure that all was well and neat in every single detail so that Bownath, his boss would be pleased, but there was always something that Bownath would find to complain about.

Bownath, the plantation owner showed up with his entire family on weekends. This family visit meant more chores for Claude. Claude would smile, but behind his smile you could visualize his broken spirit, anger, and humiliation. Claude was treated with scant courtesy, less of a person; literally as a slave. When Bownath arrived, Claude always appeared frightened and fidgety. In terms of the production of cocoa, citrus, and coffee crops, Claude was accountable to Bownath for the day to day activities, making sure that he had a good report every time.

To Jonjon, Claude's boss was overbearing and demanding. Just as Dado Ramoo, Bownath shouted to the top of his voice, making sure that everyone knew that he was around. It could be that this was the way the bourgeois controlled the proletariat; strike fear into them to keep them in line; subjugated. Colloquially it is said in Trinidad that "when your hand is in di lion mouth yuh have to pull it out easy," for fear that you might upset the lion. One should do everything possible to keep the lion at bay.

Claude's situation was tenuous, he had no choice. He had nowhere to go so he had to accept whatever was meted out to him, no matter how humiliating. Uncomfortable is an understatement to describe Claude's reactions to Bownath the landlord. Claude knew that he could not slip; he had no room for error. At least he had a place to call home for the moment on Bownath's land. Never did he smile when Bownath was around. His saddened face lasted until the boss left on Sunday afternoon. While his boss was present Claude was more or less in a "straight jacket," running here, running there, climbing, collecting fruits, and serving Bownath's full grown children at their every beck and call; there was no rest for Claude. Claude was a pitiful, saddened and depressed sight; captured because of his economic situation, dispossessed of his humanity. It was difficult to decipher whether the scenes Jonjon witnessed was a matter of respect or a question of abhorrent slavery. Jonjon wondered about what could have caused Claude to have fallen into this kind of circumstance. He asked Neeta but she told him to ignore what he saw, and counseled him to just watch and learn. In his little mind, Jonjon must have figured that maybe this was the way that laborers should be treated. It was difficult for him to envisage what he considered as torture.

There was a common name that existed between Claude and Jonjon. The name "Bankey" was their special name because Jonjon explained that he could massage anybody just like a man called Bankey. Bankey lived on Picton Street in Sangre Grande where he practiced his art in "rubbing" people. On mornings, Claude would shout out to Jonjon, "Bankey!" and Jonjon would return the greeting, "Bankey!" Assuming the role of Bankey, the man who massaged people, Jonjon's tiny hands were instrumental in massaging Claude's painful shoulder. Applying the home-made liniment comprised of Wintergreen oil, mustard oil, methylated spirit, bush rum, and coconut oil, Claude felt at least temporary relief from his pain. Not only did Jonjon massage Claude, he massaged anyone who was in pain almost every day on evenings. Dohfeh had pain in his ankles and feet, Neeta complained of pain in her right elbow, and Quero had pain at the back of his neck. Judging from the gingerly way he walked, Dohfeh could have been suffering from gouty attacks or arthritis but he was always resistant to visit any doctor. Neeta, on the other hand, could have contracted tennis elbow from the action of picking cocoa pods with a long thin bamboo rod to which a sharp cocoa knife or gullet was attached. The constant pushing and pulling with the rod could have generated the problem.

Helping out with the work load was a donkey that Claude owned. This donkey was a quiet, docile jenny. A little way beyond Neeta's land to the south, was the *whiteman's* plantation where a violent jackass and a huge mule lived. Sometimes this jackass would break his tether and gallop down the road to engage in copulatory activities with Claude's donkey. Many times the jackass would bite into the flesh of Claude's donkey. Because of his wild and violent behavior, the handlers of the donkey sometimes had no other choice but beat him off the jenny with long bamboo rods. It was the only way for him to release his vicious teeth on the hapless female. It appeared that the mule and the donkey "conversed" with each other and they both would run menacingly all over the place. Neeta was more than afraid of these beasts. Anytime she walked the lonely road up to Dohfeh's house, she walked in fear of these animals. She was vigilant to keep her eyes peeled on the half-mile strip of road and in between the cocoa and citrus fields on the lookout for this "dangerous" donkey.

Claude would come up the hill at Neeta's house to *lime* almost every evening to partake of a small meal and some hot home-made chocolate. Sometimes he would go down the hill with Boon behind the house into the cocoa field to hunt for manicou. Jonjon always wished that he could go with them. They told him that he would go with them when he got a little older. After polishing the carbide lamps' brass-finished reflector to a high luster with *Brasso* metal polish, the two hunters securely attached the lamps to their heads and the carbide canister to their belts. With a tiny but powerful flame coming through a tiny port in the middle of the reflector, these carbide head lamps shone bright as day. No manicou could hide from this light. Armed with a 16-gauge shotgun, there were times when they caught two or three manicou, sometimes they returned empty-handed, only seeing a couple big-eyed, goziey manicou (Manicou gros-yeux), a type of small opossum.

On many occasions, the moonlight was welcome, and all in the house waited in expectation of a successful hunt. Catching a couple of manicou was always an exciting moment. The grapefruit trees that surrounded the house were sometimes laden with large ripe grapefruits, which reflected the moonlight like bulbs on a Christmas tree. The moonlight facilitated the collection of dry grapefruit tree firewood to start a fire in the *chulha* situated at the top of a box drain in the yard. Neeta formed the chulha from a five gallon Norwegian butter pan using the bottom of the drain as the base. The chulha helped a lot in saving money which would be spent on propane gas for the kitchen stove. Apart from singeing manicou, chicken, ducks, and other animals, many food items, for example, roast *breadfruit*, boiled *chataigne*, roast *coconut bake* (fire on top and fire below), *cassava pone*, and boiled ham at Christmas were done to perfection on the chulha. Neeta even baked really great tasting sponge cakes inside a large iron pot on the chulha.

The noise of the night in chopping the firewood and lighting up the chulha generated a sense of friendship and togetherness among neighbors. The midnight smell of singeing a manicou and the commotion, the lighting of the *flambeau* chopping up the carcass, seasoning and partially cooking the beasts after the hunt was yet another aspect of the sense of place defined by such activities at Neeta's country house. For the sumptuous taste that Neeta's cooking provided, especially with manicou or any other wild meat, she prepared special seasonings with the proportions remaining a secret. However, Neeta used a variety of herbs including garlic, onions, peppercorns, chive, Spanish thyme, fine leaf thyme, shadon beni, and slices of fresh, hot Scotch Bonnet pepper pods. With all the ingredients formed into a heap, Neeta would *pisay* the mass of the herbal stuff with a *lorha* on a *sil* (Figure 16). In a large enamel basin, the ground up seasonings and a dash of salt and black pepper would join the chopped meat and was allowed to marinate for about an hour or so. On the little three-burner gas stove, Neeta would then *bounjay* the seasoned meat. The absence of a refrigerator was the primary reason why the meat had to be at least pre-cooked. Neeta could not afford any spoilage; meat was expensive, especially wild game. Two or three manicou could be served for the entire week along with rice and dhal, or boiled ground provisions such as dasheen, cassava, or white yams. Boiled green bananas, *tom-tom*, or steamed breadfruit also formed part of the staples.

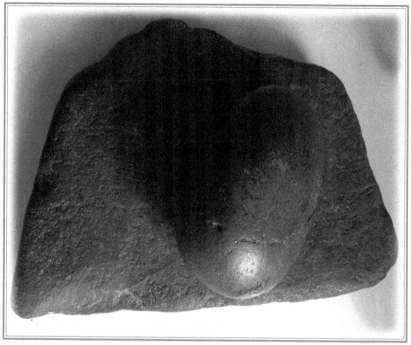

Figure 16. A sil (flat stone) and lorha (round grinding stone).
(Photo by author, 2018)

When the hunting season opened on October 01, Claude would also accompany Quero, Dohfeh, and Boon on weekend hunting trips. Their favorite hunting locations were Mafeking and Bush-Bush forests. Agouti, deer, and lappe were some of the animals they brought home. The same rituals applied in the processing of all captured game animals, and the same bragging continued up into the night, as they relived the moments how they shot each animal. Agouti was the most popular of the meats. Lappe and deer were a rare treat. These men would hunt for the entire season which ended on the last day of February. Sometimes there would be four to six agouti on the cleaning table. After they were singed, Neeta took care of all of them.

Used in the chase were two to four beagle hound dogs. Quero owned two really young, powerful, and active dogs, "Shortboy" and "Pepsi." They were dogs of good pedigree. These dogs were so good that during their early hunting experience they chased a buck until they "penned" it. Quero took the shot and approximately 80 pounds of venison fell at his feet. The deer in Trinidad is a small type known as red brocket deer. Shortboy and Pepsi were kept in separate kennels that were always locked. However there was one day when disaster struck. With their zeal and power, and the instinct to hunt and kill, they forced the door of their kennels and broke free when no one was around.

Apparently, the freedom that the chickens enjoyed around Neeta's house bothered the dogs. That fateful day, the dogs chased and slew about 120 chickens; they had a field day. A few of the chickens escaped. When Neeta arrived to feed the dogs and the chickens she was more angry than heartbroken for one of the sources of her income just about vanished. To her this was bad luck at work, destroying her efforts at creating wealth. In her upset state, she went about searching for her dead chickens that filled three large crocus bags. Processing the chickens was the next ordeal she had to undergo. Neeta and Quero were both upset, but what could they do? Hurriedly Quero packed the trunk of the car with the carcasses and they quickly made their way home on Oropouche Road to begin the cleaning of the chickens.

Neeta was mad as a raging bull; incensed. After boiling a huge pot of water for soaking the chickens she stood in front of the kitchen sink for well over four hours plucking, gutting, chopping, separating, and bagging every chicken for storage in the freezer space she rented from the grocer where she sold her common fowl eggs. Quero did not help her, but he had *common fowl* meat to eat almost every day for about two or three months. The house smelled like a chicken processing depot for days. Such things do happen; hunting dogs are bred to hunt. In Trinidad, there is a saying: "Yuh cyar play mas if yuh 'fraid powder." The surviving chickens served to raise another huge flock.

With the new clutch of pullets and roosters clucking, crowing, and scratching around, Jonjon had the odious task of cleaning up the yard around the country house, and the chickens did not help him. He had to remove several stinky, bunches of half-rotted, fly-infested, half-eaten bunches of Mysore bananas that Neeta left around as a feed supplement for her chickens. Not only that, but he had to, with a hoe and shovel, scrape off the chicken droppings that dotted the yard. Soon enough, the removal of the chicken poop was no longer his work. He noticed that the droppings were quite scanty when he came out to clean the yard.

It appeared that Neeta's newly acquired "pot hound" puppy was having a feast. That dog relished the taste of chicken poop. Neeta *"paytayed"* for him behind the house as he sneakily licked the chicken crap from off the ground. Caught in the act, Neeta held him down with his little nose pressed into a load of the filth and delivered a good "cut tail" on him as she simultaneously christened him *"Caca Mange."* Nevertheless, Caca Mange, so used to his habit, continued to eat fowl droppings on a daily basis. In Trinidad, the saying goes, "When dog sucking egg, dey always sucking egg." It seems that this statement applies to everything including chicken poop. Despite his habits and misfortune with floggings and rebuffs, Caca Mange welcomed Claude and everyone else to his home up the hill. Claude would call out to him, "Caca Mange!" and he would come running down the hill madly wagging his tail.

No one was actually privy to Claude's trials, his pains, his suffering, his de-humanization or his dire economic circumstances. He talked little, sometimes expressionless and Neeta did not pry into his affairs. However, for a few dollars, there were times when Claude would offer to give Neeta a "pull out" (a little help) with the harvesting of bananas. On Thursdays of every week Neeta sold bananas to the government-owned Marketing Board, otherwise known as the Control Board. As a former British colonial establishment, the office and storage facilities of the Marketing Board were located adjacent to the Civic Center and the Public Transport Service Corporation (PTSC) bus station on Brierley Street, Sangre Grande. The board offered guaranteed prices for certain species of bananas for what was believed to be part of the banana shipment to Europe.

Jonjon could see the trickery in Neeta's eyes as she cut the banana bunches with extremely long stems with the net aim to derive the heaviest weights possible for each bunch. Much to her chagrin, her dreams of making a few cents more with the supposed weights of the long stems were constantly dashed to pieces every week because the buying agent took out his knife and de-stemmed every bunch before weighing. Jonjon could see her countenance filled with disgust for the buyer, and her sighs of defiance said it all. There were times when she tried to convince the buyer to pay for all bunches but much to her disappointment, damaged ones were left as rejects. Out of this money, Claude received a dollar or two.

Eventually, it became quite noticeable that Claude had begun courting a young woman. Soon enough, he quietly got married to Neeta's niece. Unbeknownst to Neeta, Claude was dating Angela for a long time now but Neeta was not surprised about Angela's hostile ways. Angela never greeted Neeta or even said hello on her arrival at Claude's abode. Within a couple of years Diedre was born, but Neeta never got the chance to hold the baby. In her father's arms, Diedre came up the hill for the first time when she was about two years old. Who knows what bad blood and rancor existed between Neeta and Angela's forbears? Although Neeta sent treats and food to the family, Angela refused to greet Neeta. The coldness remained until Claude left the premises.

In due course, Bownath fell ill with a debilitating stroke. He could not talk, and walking became more and more tedious for him. His loud voice was quieted and his presumptuous strutting around ceased. Neeta counseled Jonjon about Bownath's misfortune stating that a person could do as much as he wanted but not as long as he wanted. On this note, she should have spoken to herself. She should have remembered that monkeys always see the length of the other monkey's tail; they never see theirs. Having been struck by such an illness, Bownath decided to dispose of his property. In light of the sale, Claude had to vacate the premises. Just a little distance from the Manzanilla Road junction, Claude acquired an allotment and managed somehow to build a makeshift dwelling for his little family on Kowlessur Road. A couple of times afterwards, Claude greeted Jonjon on his way to Neeta's. Then suddenly, Claude was no longer present on the landscape; Claude died. Sad as it was, Jonjon lost a friend, a really good friend. Because of his infectious laughter, the village mourned his loss for quite some time, especially at Christmastime.

At about this time in his life, Jonjon had already completed at least four years at high school. He had gained entrance and enrolled to read for the University of Cambridge General Certificate of Education (GCE) at Northeastern College in Sangre Grande. One pleasant Saturday evening, almost as every other Saturday evening when he walked up on Kowlessur Road on his way to Neeta's house, he encountered someone who troubled his little mind.

As he turned the bend around Flemo's house he noticed two teenaged girls walking a little way off in front of him. In the dying hours of the day, Jonjon walked briskly behind them but crossed the road to the right side when he came closer to them. He did not want to alarm the girls by "creeping" up on them. As he crossed the road, one of the girls, the shorter of the two, glanced furtively at him. He knew that she was looking, maybe with the intent to "scope" him out. She was a pretty girl with long flowing hair that shone in the evening sunshine. Jonjon arrived at his destination at Neeta's up the hill amidst the grapefruit trees. Down the hill there appeared to be a new owner of the property, and the said girl, who had looked at him, was walking into the yard. Jonjon assumed that the girl was the daughter of the landlord.

As Jonjon entered the country house, he scarcely had a moment to greet Neeta when she interjected that he had to get ready quickly to attend dinner at the house down the hill. With the sun-warmed water contained in the barrel next to the house, Jonjon hastily took a bath and donned his best clothes. The new owners were celebrating their new acquisition with a thanksgiving. Jonjon dressed for the occasion with a grey silk shirt, black trousers, and black leather shoes. He looked dapper and ready to take on the world. In the bright light of the *Coleman* gas lamps, Jonjon realized he was not alone at the long trestle table where he was invited to sit. There were several young and handsome men sitting with him, but it seemed that Ranu, the girl he had encountered earlier in that evening, was showing him some special attention much to the annoyance of the other fellows.

By ignoring the other young men, it seemed as though Ranu was instructed to attend to Jonjon alone. "Would you like some more food?" she asked him, but Jonjon was too nervous to reply. He just smiled and shook his head to say "No." The food was the typical meatless, East Indian "prayers food" consisting of white rice, dhal, curried *channa* and *aloo*, bhagi, curried chataigne, pumpkin, and black sweet peppery masala mango served on a *sohari* or *kashiboo* leaf. Having had his fill, Jonjon decided to make room for another invitee to sit in his place, but that was not to be. As he rose to exit the table, Ranu quickly returned with an offering of sweet rice (rice pudding). "Would you like some?" Speechless, he once again shook his head from side to side indicating that he did not want any sweet rice. He was not a lover of the treat. Although he refused her offering, she insisted, "but I made it myself and it tastes really good" stressing her interest in Jonjon's acceptance. Bewitched by her smile, her tender voice, cuteness, and the twinkle in her eyes, Jonjon acquiesced to her bidding and swallowed the sweet morsel, cherry on top and all.

The following day (Sunday), while the dew still lingered on the grass on the edges of the muddy path that led down from the house into the cocoa field, Neeta and Jonjon took an early strike at picking some cocoa pods. Jonjon's job was to *samblay* every pod that Neeta dislodged from every tree. While she picked the pods, she counted every one, as well as noting the location of each one that fell. Neeta harvested every pod, no matter how high and seemingly out of reach; Neeta sometimes partially climbed the tree to get to the pods. That woman was relentless! Dragging a heavy crocus bag along, Jonjon's task was to find every pod that hid in the tall *gamalot* grass. This was not nice work because the blades of the grass had sharp edges that bruised his arms. He was little, short for a boy of his age. For a child of this structure, this type of activity was a bit demanding. Jonjon resented the toil and labor he had to endure as a child in his godmother's cocoa estate.

After the collection of the pods, frightful as it was, he had to walk by himself a little way off to empty his bag on the newly formed heap of cocoa pods. This was tiring and disgusting for him. He was cautious not to go too near the *bodaage*, the border or transition zone between boundaries. Neeta warned that there could be venomous snakes like the *mapipire* hiding in the bodaage. Why did he have to do all this hard and miserable work? This was the only question he asked himself. Nevertheless, Neeta had a task to complete, and by hook or crook, she was bent on raking in every cocoa bean.

Many of the ancient tall cocoa trees that were probably planted since the days of the Santa Estrella Estate bore only a few pods. At this time in the year, Neeta collected only the *raebuk*, the one or two pods that were ripe. She would say that if she did not get the pods the squirrels would eventually get them, and she wanted every bean! There were several pests and diseases that were deleterious to good cocoa yields. Squirrels were everywhere. Then there were two bad diseases, *Black Pod* disease, and *Witches Broom* disease. Squirrels, Black Pod, and Witches Broom could severely damage or totally ruin a cocoa plantation. What was a bit bothersome for Jonjon was the fact that Neeta would at times jump the boundaries of adjacent lands to pick a row or two of another person's cocoa trees. Ignoring the presence of the *ryo* boundary plants (Dracaena cane plants); Neeta stole cocoa pods from other people's holdings with impunity! In his mind, Jonjon questioned, "Why would she do this? What am I doing here?" Neeta couldn't care; she was the type to reap where she did not sow; she was a thief without any conscience, plain and simple. Moreover she stole as one without regard for anyone. Her determination to take someone else's property was appalling; disgusting. Without a choice, Jonjon just went along, but his mind was beginning to turn away from wanting to stay anymore with Neeta; he was fed up with her shenanigans.

The day drew on and the humidity and heat of the cocoa field rose to a scale of intolerance. Lunchtime came and Neeta decided to stop the cocoa-picking activity. Tired, sweaty, sticky, speechless and frustrated, Jonjon inched his way on the muddy track up to the country house. He realized that this type of work was not what he wanted to do for the rest of his life. He could not see himself being like this throughout his life. Thinking deeply about the situation, he determined in his heart to make good his studies at Northeastern College; to be successful in all his examinations, yes, to lift himself out of the morass of hardship and poverty. At least he formed a mindset to do better.

Despite his toil and struggle that Sunday, Jonjon did not forget about Ranu and her hints of affection towards him the night before. Flashes of her smile and beautiful eyes, her long, light shining hair played upon his mind at intervals but he mused that this was just a dream that toyed with his mind. He was dreaming big time. The castles he constructed in the air could come crashing down at any moment. Ranu interfered with his mind and infected his soul and although getting close to her was an absent reality, he cherished the thought that there still could be hope; where there is life there is hope.

By the time he got to the house, Jonjon faced the reality that he might never have the opportunity to see Ranu again. Hope gave way to despair. He was depressed. Nevertheless, there is a saying, "Weeping endures for the night, but joy comes in the morning." As a corollary to this statement, Jonjon remembers a couple of lines from his elementary school reading book: "The darkest watch of night is the one before the dawn, but relief is always nearest when we least expect it."

In his despondency and childhood confusion, Jonjon lingered in the shade of the grapefruit trees that flanked the southern hillside of the house. Suddenly he heard a faint chatter of voices down the hill in the road. Standing on the grassy path between the grapefruit trees that led to the road where bananas were stacked for sale he saw Ranu and her friend "loitering," kicking pebbles in the road. They seemed bored and were probably wondering what to do next. Jonjon did not hesitate to call out to the girls. With a broad welcoming smile Ranu responded to Jonjon as he greeted the girls. Ranu was exuberant, totally bubbly in welcoming Jonjon. "What are you two doing here," he asked. "We were thinking about going for a walk but we do not know the place too well," Ranu explained. "Do you know this area? Will you go for a walk with us?" "O yes! We can all have a nice walk. It's such a nice sunny day," Jonjon was quick to affirm.

In seconds, the three started off to walk southwards in the shelter and shade of the forested area that Neeta owned on the stretch of road that led to the entry gate of the whiteman's property. On reaching the turn in the road on the left that led downhill, Ranu's friend motioned that she was no longer interested in taking the walk and strolled back to the house. Jonjon surmised that it was a bit fishy, or weird that she suddenly decided to leave Ranu with him. Was this some kind of plot? Anyway, the two continued walking and talking. Sometimes there was silence, not knowing what to say.

Unbeknownst to Neeta, Jonjon stole away, not caring about lunch anymore, and certainly not tired. He was with Ranu and nothing else mattered. They walked past the laborer's barracks where old man Deo lived. They both waved to Deo and kept on walking. It was a hot and humid day, with little intermittent zephyrs. Eventually they reached the crest of the hill to the cocoa house where Dohfeh resided. Jonjon was careful not to go beyond that point in the road. He could have taken her around the bend down a few hundred yards to the other side of the hill to show her where Ma Romany lived, but he reasoned that they had walked too far already. At the top of the hill they stood and took in the view of the lush valley below to the south, all part of the whiteman's holdings. After the pause they started on the trek back home.

Ranu appeared quite happy with her little "expedition." She smiled constantly. Her angelic voice was music to Jonjon's ears. She was a delight to behold. Her long hair accepted the breeze with glee blowing all over her face with some of the strands sticking to her face; simply beautiful. Coming down the semi-paved asphalt surface was a bit treacherous for one who was only wearing a slipper. Part of the asphalt was scaled off, exposing the sub-structure of gravel. With the problem of controlling her speed on the loose gravelly surface Jonjon offered to take Ranu's hand to prevent her from falling. From that point onwards, she did not let go of his hand. His heart pounded in his chest. It probably reached his throat. His speech mechanism was now defunct. It was a bit awkward for him but it felt good to know that he was holding her soft hands; yes, it felt so good!

On reaching the point from whence they started, Jonjon and Ranu stopped a few feet from the crest of the hill that was shielded from the view of others on both sides of the road by high cut banks. No one could have seen them there. In fact, they were too short for anyone to have seen them. They stood there speechless, staring dreamy-eyed and tenderly at each other. There was a kind of unearthly tension. The only witnesses were the grapefruit trees, laden with yellow ripe fruits and the tall forest trees that stood above on Neeta's land. Literally trembling, they drew closer and closer to each other with nothing more than electricity filling the space between them. Helplessly they fell into each other's arms and sealed their love with a mouth-watering kiss. Losing track of time and space, Ranu asked Jonjon to kiss her again, "Please kiss me again, please..." Jonjon did not grant her that wish but said: "I will kiss you when we meet again." They said their goodbyes and Jonjon ran up the track to Neeta's house. He was happy and excited beyond measure. Many years after, while reminiscing about the encounter, Jonjon wrote the poem below:

Johnny Coomansingh

...the grapefruit tree

As the sun dipped low
Kissing the trees; iridescent glow
I walked past you on a country path
In that moment you stole my heart.

As you walked that day in the evening sun
Your hair I saw as golden spun
Light and free it draped your waist
Seeing your glory, my heart hastened its pace.

One little gaze,
Left in a daze
I could not ever erase
For fourteen thousand, six hundred days!

And after such a nervous mile
With a never-ending smile
Offered me the sweetest rice
So gentle, so humble, so nice...

In my soul I knew...
Strong, it was, my love for you
Restless, so full of torment,
My racing heart would not relent!

But the sun for another day
Summoned all creatures to dance, to sing, to play,
And we walked for too long a time
Many-a-hill did we climb.

And on that sun-drenched day
We had little to say
On the final hill
We stood still...

Gazing into the hazel-eyed fire
Wallowing, perhaps whimpering in a pool of desire
Within a hair's breadth in a moment of bliss
Stained our lips in the first mouth-watering kiss.

Nervous, yet motionless, we stood on that spot
And from my mind I could not blot
From my soul, the joy, the ecstasy,
Witnessed only by the grapefruit tree.

It was way past lunchtime and Neeta was out and about doing chores. Jonjon did not eat much of a lunch, some rice and salmon stewed with tomato was the fare. His mind was racing, jubilant, too excited to think of anything else but his beautiful Ranu. Neeta suspected that something had happened to him but she did not ask a question. As the evening drew on, everyone washed up and began getting ready for a light dinner of creole chocolate tea, sada roti and the rest of the salmon, Jonjon related to Neeta his love for Ranu. Without any hesitation, Neeta firmly told him to forget about Ranu. She explained: "Ranu is a girl from 'down below'...she is a town girl and she does not have to study you.... and her father will not want a poor boy like you for his only daughter. Stop dreaming. Forget about that girl." Neeta's words fell like acid on his heart, like salt on a crapaud's back; they were unbearable, sickening. A million thoughts flashed through his mind about Ranu and what Neeta hinted. The opportunity to kiss Ranu again never came. Jonjon felt like kicking himself. He should have granted her wish. He thought to himself, "O what a fool I was!"

Days turned into weeks, weeks turned into months and he did not see Ranu ever again. Apparently she told her father about her love for Jonjon, and for that reason, her father prevented her from returning to Kowlessur Road. Jonjon felt lost, possessed of a spirit that could not be satisfied. He so badly wanted to see Ranu for one last time, but there were difficulties and obstacles, chief of which was his poverty. Why was he so poor! Without money to travel, he had to accept the fact that he would never see Ranu again, the love of his life. At school his thoughts would dither just thinking about how much he wanted to be with her. No one knew his feelings, his utter mental destitution. The encounter with Ranu left him broken, and the words Neeta said to him played on his mind like a stuck long playing record: "She is from down below," dissonant words that he did not want to hear.

Despite his feelings and probable loss, Jonjon came up as usual to Neeta's every Saturday evening. On this particular evening Jonjon planned to give to Neeta a taste of her own medicine; a jumbie lesson. The sun was setting and the cocoa field was beginning to darken. Remembering her superstitious ways, he decided to frighten her. He knew from discussions before that she would be down in the flats picking cocoa. She told him to meet her there when he came up. Jonjon just couldn't go down into the cocoa field with just his normal "cocoa clothes." He had other plans. With a big old straw hat on his head and wearing an old musty gent's jacket that covered him almost to his ankles, Jonjon went down slowly down the hill into the cocoa field.

About one hundred feet from the flats, there was a big *moubeh* tree. Neeta could not see too well so Jonjon decided to hide behind the tree and slowly show himself at intervals in the bushy track crying, "whoop, whoop, whoop," the alleged sound of a duenne. Neeta looked up the hill and saw a figure shifting back and forth from behind the tree. Then she stopped and took a good look. In a flash she dropped the cocoa rod and ran in the opposite direction. When Jonjon saw her plight, rather her flight, he yelled out, "Aye, aye, it's me! It's me!" Neeta was quite plump, and for a woman of her size, she was actually flying through the bush. There was nothing in this world that could have caught up with her. She ran pell-mell, and forgetting the bridge, she capsized into the cocoa canal; she could have drowned. Neeta was angry, soaked to the skin, scared stiff, but Jonjon fell to his knees laughing. His laughter was uncontrollable. After composing herself, Neeta shouted, "Yuh damn little scamp! Yuh playing duenne? Ah go fix yuh!" Jonjon exacted upon Neeta what she used to do to him when he was much younger. Neeta ended up laughing with Jonjon. Work ended immediately. This was one of Jonjon's more interesting moments with Neeta.

CHAPTER SIX

"It is not the man who has little, but he who desires more, that is poor" (Seneca)

Dancing di cocoa...hoarding every cent!

DECEMBER COMES AROUND and so do the harvests of the cocoa and coffee crops. The cocoa harvesting activity was Jonjon's nemesis. Harvesting cocoa, especially the breaking or cracking of the pods meant pain, disgust, and utter discomfort for Jonjon. What was he to do? How could he escape? He found himself in the clutches of Neeta's drive to make money, to rake up every bean, to avariciously catch every penny.

Early on Sunday morning Neeta would rise to cook a meal of white rice, dhal, and curried chicken. To prevent spillage, the enamel pots of rice, dhal, and chicken were tied up firmly with cotton cloths and packed in a cocoa basket. Watercress, cucumbers, and tomatoes accompanied the meal. After making a *karat*, a circular pad constructed from dried banana leaves, Boon placed the pad on his head to receive the cocoa basket with the food. Down the muddy, slippery path he nervously trod with the precious victuals needed for lunch on top of his head. As he walked, he was ever reminded by Saga to be careful. Saga repeated, "Take care boi, doh fall dey nah...yuh have to take care with di dhal boi. Watch the dhal boi." Saga loved Neeta's yellow split peas dhal and drank himself a cupful at lunchtime. By all standards, it was certainly the best dhal ever; boiled, seasoned, and *chunkayed* to perfection. A *kalchool* containing hot, garlic infused vegetable oil is used to chunkay dhal. The kalchool is normally immersed in the pot of dhal with the emittance of a sizzling noise.

As the company, including Quero, made their way to the biggest heap of cocoa pods that anyone could have seen. Jonjon did not feel any desire to be part of such a group. His repulsion of the task ahead grew exponentially. Internally, he resented the cracking of cocoa, not to mention the pain in his fingers that followed. The two or three days needed to complete the cocoa-cracking process were like a lifetime of torture for him. Sometimes the rains came and he would be soaked to the skin. His little fingers would become crimpled and white because of the cold. Neeta's remedy for the cold was a quick small shot of bush rum. A cork full of the rum would hit the back of the throat and in less than a millisecond, the action of the rum would be felt. Jonjon would feel as though there was a fire in in his throat with smoke coming through his ears. In his mind the questions remained; no answers given.

Several heavy bags of wet cocoa would soon grace the roadside next to the pile of green bananas stacked for sale to the Marketing Board. The toting of cocoa was Boon's job. Jonjon carried the plastic one gallon water bottles and other miscellaneous items in a cocoa basket up the hill to the house. Although tired and grumpy, late in the evenings, after plying his taxi for hire, Quero would pick up the bags of wet cocoa for delivery to Dohfeh's fermentation box (sweat box). Neeta had a small drying house which was not large enough for the huge quantity of cocoa and coffee beans she harvested. In fact, she used her drying house for the coffee beans she had harvested a couple weeks before. Also, she did not have a fermentation box. Seven or eight days later, the fermented cocoa beans would be moved upstairs into Dohfeh's drying house. Fermented cocoa is hot and steamy but this process is extremely important to impart a better tasting chocolate.

Before getting into the activities for the day, Neeta cautioned Jonjon to take an early bath because she did not want him to catch a cold if he had to bathe after cleaning the hot cocoa. After the bath she told him to rub his hands and feet with coconut oil to prevent the cocoa slime from sticking to him. Literally working as a mule, Boon hauled the hot cocoa, basket after basket, up a flight of stairs about twenty feet high. Leaving enough space to walk around, Boon dumped the cocoa in heaps all over the cedar wood drying floor. Every heap of the hot cocoa contained large balls of cocoa called "bull." Double beans, beans that stuck together were also present. The bulls and double beans had to be broken into single beans. In essence, during the drying process all beans had to be single beans, provided the proprietor wanted a better price.

Along with Neeta, Jonjon sat on a *peerha* and faced heap after heap of steamy hot cocoa beans. His job was to separate the beans and remove trash from the fermented hot cocoa. The constant heat of the cocoa hitting his face was very unpleasant, the smell, "unkind." Cleaning out the hot cocoa was just as unpleasant as cracking and cleaning out the pods in the field. Apparently, in the cocoa business this was the repulsive type of work prescribed for little children. After cleaning out all the heaps, the beans would be spread on the cedar-wood drying floor. The roof of the drying house would be pushed back to accommodate the raging sunshine every day. Because of the tropical weather that exists in Trinidad, drying cocoa requires acute vigilance; don't ever fall off to sleep. Rain could fall at the drop of a hat and the extra water would not only spoil the beans, but all the rooms and their contents below the drying floor could get soaked. Drying the beans took much time and Neeta would be up at Dohfeh's at the crack of dawn. Some days were hot and dry and the heat of the day contributed to a modicum of laziness that Jonjon experienced on quite a few occasions during the cocoa drying activities. There was almost nothing to do but listen to the songbirds or go digging in strange places to find things. Hot and humid weather causes strange behavior in people.

During his knocking around and digging activities Jonjon stumbled upon a strange looking hole at the northern corner pillar of Dohfeh's house. In the hole were bits of rock, stones, wire and cloth, indeed a bizarre find. Like a dog after a buried bone, Jonjon removed all the debris until he came upon a covered Milo tin under a layer of fine red sand. What was this tin doing there buried beneath the sand? Suddenly from out of the bush Dohfeh came running and shouting, "Put that down! Put that down! Put it down!" Astonished at his reaction, Jonjon put the tin right where he found it. Dohfeh came up to him and asked furiuosly: "Why yuh went digging dey boi? Yuh put something dey? Allyuh chirren good yes." Although he looked furious, his countenance changed almost immediately to a sneaky smile and picked up the tin. Neeta was quick to ask: "Wuh yuh have in dat tin dey Dohfeh?" He replied: "Dat is none ah yuh business. Yuh too *farse*." She jokingly fought him a little bit for the tin but he escaped and ran inside his house. Later that evening he opened the tin and showed Jonjon and Neeta a roll of several one hundred dollar bills that were stashed in the hole. Dohfeh had gotten there in time. If he had not caught Jonjon at that moment, Neeta would have surely taken a few bills. Dohfeh never used any banking institution until that day. After talking with Neeta, the next day Quero took him to the bank to open an account. With some of the money he also bought a divan sitting room suite and a pro-gas stove. Before that, the only items he had in his house were two beds and a hammock.

In the almost still, windless environment, Jonjon heard the "blee-blee, blee-blee" call of the cravat songbirds perched way up high on the leafless branches of the rubber trees that flanked the hilly southern side of Dohfeh's plantation. The dry rubber trees were ring-barked and were just standing there, falling off piece by piece. Combined with the pleasant tones of the birds, Jonjon also heard the cackle of sandbox and rubber seed capsules in the distance as they exploded in the hot blazing sun. He wondered how to cage one of these birds. In his childlike innocence, Jonjon asked Neeta if there was a possibility of him getting one of these birds in a cage. Neeta described the difficulty with catching these birds when she said, "The only way to catch those birds is to *"floneer"* the cage with a rope and pull up the cage until it reached the height where the birds are located. These birds are hard to catch." Jonjon thought about Neeta's suggestion but did not pursue the cravat. Catching a cravat required skill, and where would he get that quantity of rope to floneer a cage? If he couldn't cage a bird or go catch some fish in a cocoa canal, there wasn't much for a little boy to do when cocoa was drying except to turn the beans upstairs on the drying floor.

Jonjon's designated task was to walk through the beans to turn them as they dried. When the beans became drier, he used a *rabo*, a flat piece of cedar wood affixed to a thin strong bamboo pole, to turn the beans. Basically, the rabo is a rake without tines. Walking through the beans amounted to a sort of shuffling action with the feet without crushing even one bean. As Jonjon shuffled the beans, slimy clumps of cocoa refuse clung to his feet and ankles. He disliked this aspect of cocoa drying. In fact, he disliked every phase involved in the production of cocoa. Resentment for his "enslavement" grew rapidly and uncontrollably as he contemplated how to break free from the shackles of the rounds of toil that comprised cocoa production. Knowing that he was working for just a plate of food and that not one penny would be shared with him, Jonjon asked himself whether this was the type of work that he wanted to be saddled with for the rest of his life. The answer came back crystal clear. "No!" Neeta had no clue about the musings in Jonjon's mind. Jonjon was beginning to view the world differently. Little by little, he realized that he was just one of the cogs in Neeta's production wheel in her efforts to create her fortune. His labor, however insignificant, was there only to funnel money into her bank account. His payment was food. He was working for nothing more but food!

Patience is virtue, and the day would come in the week just before Christmas for "dancing di cocoa;" the final act in preparation of the beans before bagging. Dohfeh was an expert at dancing cocoa. Was it a real dance? Maybe yes, maybe no, but it appeared that an individual had to become a sort of a ninja to dance cocoa. After sprinkling the heap of dried cocoa with a mixture of the slimy juice of *bois canot* leaves, fresh coconut oil, and water, Dohfeh would roll up his blue-dock trousers and get into the heap. As though in a trance, literally floating, becoming as it were, lighter in weight, he polished the beans without crushing one bean for about 15-20 minutes. This was the cocoa dance and everyone rejoiced. The hard, menial and trying work was over and Christmas was in the air. Spreading out the beans to dry a little more, Neeta would serve up a mouth-watering chicken *pelau* cooked on Dohfeh's fireside located in his muddied outside kitchen where a couple of setting hens could be seen in the corners of the small makeshift hovel. One or two pounds of freshly picked pigeon peas would go into making the pelau. The smoke of the fireside rendered the pelau exceptionally tasty; a good country taste, not to mention the *bun-bun*, the charred remnants at the bottom of the pot. Nothing tasted better than pelau bun-bun. To wash down the pelau, Neeta provided freshly squeezed ice-cold orange juice.

When the beans were fully dried, Neeta and Dohfeh used a wooden shovel to fill the blue-seam crocus bags and sewed them up with a cocoa needle and thick sisal twine. Five or six bags were now ready for the cocoa store. At the cocoa store, the buyer would knock or slap the side of the bags to hear if the beans rattled. If he heard a pleasant dry rattle he knew that the beans were of the quality required for export. It was the same test for the coffee beans only that coffee did not require "dancing" or polishing. However, to fetch a better price, many coffee producers preferred to hull their coffee before sale. There were two coffee hulling mills in Sangre Grande, one near to Goat Hill and the other on Cunaripo Road.

After the sale of the cocoa, Neeta gave not a penny to anyone neither did she show her gratitude to all those who helped her bring in the crop. She hoarded every cent! Jonjon knew that his time with Neeta was coming to an end. He explained the situation with slaving for Neeta to his mother and not long afterwards he was prevented from returning to Neeta's country house. Despite his mother's command, Neeta and Quero still showed up at Jonjon's Adventist Street home, and even at the close of church service to take him along, but his mother said "No." They actually begged his mom for him to come along because as Neeta said, "I only want him around for ah lil company in the country house." "Jonjon is not going anywhere!" his mother answered firmly. Despite the fact that his family was poor and struggling to survive, Neeta got the message and eventually accepted the fact that Jonjon was not someone to be used anymore for her personal gain. Boon remained and slaved for her until he was eighteen. When Boon was much younger, Neeta made an effort to send him to school but on advice of Mamo, his mother, his father came and took him away from Neeta. Mamo once stated: "Mama eh know, papa eh know, *chile* eh bong tuh know…he go live." Boon stayed with his parents for a few months but not long after he returned to Neeta as a "slave." Thereafter, his life was nothing else but hard labor. Maybe that was the mentality of the cocoa estate life and culture in those days.

Many were the experiences that Jonjon acquired while staying with Neeta. Neeta believed in obeah and while she denied it openly, covertly she indulged in certain practices that involved some aspect of obeah, for example, making small crosses with *cocoyea* tied up with black thread, maintaining a night pot of stale urine under her bed, impaling a blue colored bottle in her garden, walking backward to the door of the house at nighttime and collecting all manner of potions, powders, and weird stuff such as the dried epithelial tissue of chicken gizzards in a jar. The little crosses were stuck up on doors and windows to ward off evil, at least so she believed. At one time, Dohfeh even remarked to Jonjon: "Dat woman eh good nah." Jonjon had no idea why he deduced such an assessment of Neeta. Jonjon reasoned that it could have been Neeta's obsession with Dohfeh's plantation; the envy was manifest. Neeta coveted Dohfeh's plantation because his plantation, although of lesser acreage, produced a much higher volume of cocoa per acre. Neeta was not contented with what she had.

Gone are the glad days of bathing in the cold waters of a cocoa canal or at the little spring in Bownath's plantation, of hunting manicou, of fishing for chatto under a culvert, of catching the brown manicou crab in the cocoa field after a thunderstorm, of stomping around in the shallow recesses of the Sangre Chiquito River looking for crayfish hiding in the half-rotten bamboo stems that fell into the river, of climbing a sugar-apple (*kashema*) tree laden with ripened fruit and eating to one's heart content, and of finding a love on a country road amidst an orchard of grapefruit trees with yellow fruits glowing in the summer sunshine. Jonjon could also remember picking up small table mangoes from under the trees that flourished alongside the bridle road on the whiteman's estate.

Jonjon vividly recalls the early morning while dew still graced the southern grassy path up to Neeta's when Ramsingh dressed only in a boxer shorts and merino, with a cracker-dull in his hand, came running bare-footed up the hill to the country house screaming at the top of his voice, "Mister Francois, Mister Francois, Help! Help! O Gawd! O Gawd! Help! Somebody want tuh kill mih!" Shaking violently with fear, Ramsingh explained in a saccadic manner that there was a man hiding somewhere behind the donkey shed with a long knife. There was more to the story. According to Neeta, the man with the knife was quite likely a former lover of Ramsingh's wife. Who knows what he wanted to do that morning? Apparently, the intruder traversed miles of forest and cocoa cultivation overnight to arrive at Ramsingh's house. *Tabanca* or unrequited love does many things to people and maybe this man behind the donkey shed just wanted to have a glimpse of his lost lover.

Ramsingh was the overseer of the whiteman's property which comprised several hundred acres that bounded with Neeta's land to the north. Ramsingh stayed at Neeta for a while to regain his composure. Dohfeh (Mister Francois) accompanied him on his way back to his house and everything seemed to be alright after that encounter. Nothing more was heard about the incident concerning the man with the knife behind the donkey shed. Years after that incident, Jonjon unraveled the true context of the story, but that's another story, a very long story for another time.

Not long after, Jonjon became too occupied with his studies at Northeastern College to attend to Neeta's foreboding needs and the toil in her cocoa fields. Although he learned much about property (cocoa estate) management, for example, how to grow bananas, coffee, cocoa, citrus, and miscellaneous fruit trees, Jonjon was not "excited" anymore with serving Neeta's needs as a child slave. He needed to study, to strike out in life, to find a path to follow, to forge a future. On her ever-present quest to create more wealth, Neeta was not interested in helping Jonjon. She hoarded every penny, and scraped up every cent! She was not interested in his welfare and did not buy even a pair of school shoes for him. What she wanted was a little slave and he reasoned that what she did to Berry and Boon she was not going to do to him; he had to find a way to escape from the "shackles."

With regard to Boon, Neeta treated him with utter disrespect. She humiliated Boon to the max! In both patois and the English language, she berated him with expletives of every genre. With all certainty, if "cussing" could have killed anyone, Boon would have died a long time ago. Boon suffered the worst verbal and physical atrocities that any child could ever withstand. Boon received a little money from Neeta and one day he showed Jonjon his bank book. He had eighteen dollars and a few cents, the money he managed to save over a two-year period. Jonjon was shocked and wondered what type of demon Neeta was. How could she be so cruel to children? Why was it so difficult for her to love and understand others? It was all about her, and her drive to make money.

After an incident at Warden Road, Jonjon went into silent rebellion against Neeta. This incident was probably the one that broke the proverbial camel's back. Quero accompanied Neeta on this "expedition" to her brother's plantation. Her drive that day was to collect as many plants and ground provisions she could have transported in Quero's new Ford Zephyr. There were no shops or cafés on Warden Road where someone could buy any snacks or foodstuff. Neeta brought only a few *Crix* crackers with the thought that Mamo, her sister-in-law would have provided her with a meal. Even if her sister-in-law had prepared food, Jonjon would not have eaten. The house where Mamo lived was not conducive to human living; it was filthy! The latrine was too close to the hovel for comfort, and houseflies were everywhere; it was squalor in its greatest array. Jonjon became hungry and it was so bad, he fainted for lack of food.

After he regained consciousness, he began vomiting the few "tie-tongue" berries he ate, berries that fell by the roadside from the "Lay-lay" tree. His system went into reverse. He became sick and weakened. Neeta panicked and went straight to Ma Johnnie's house where Jonjon sipped a cup of hot ginger tea prepared for him in a flash. He was given a piece of bread and margarine to eat which helped ease his hunger. Neeta was too busy collecting banana and breadfruit plants and other items for her plantation. Coming back to her roots at Warden Road, Neeta was like a child in a candy store, forgetting what mattered most. She forgot about Jonjon and his need for a morsel of food. This experience shook Jonjon to his senses and he decided there and then never to go back to Neeta's. Nevertheless, Jonjon's heart was soft and when he grew older he indeed paid a visit to Neeta. The visit was not as cordial as he would have hoped.

CHAPTER SEVEN

A fool and his money are soon parted

Something in the mortar beside the pestle

THERE IS A saying that some people accumulate wealth for accumulation sake. If there was anybody in the world who succinctly followed that rule it was Neeta. Neeta had the true *rulebook* for making money and she knew how to use people. She wanted more money, more land, house, the best car, anything that could have given her greater prominence, status, and an edge over Quero, his sisters, and her neighbors and relatives. Neeta wanted all of them to look up to her. Her aim was to prove her detractors wrong. She always complained about her sisters-in-law. She would say to Quero at times, "Yuh sister and dem feel that dey better than mih. Ah go show all ah dem that me eh want nutten from anybody. Ah know yuh mudder eh like mih, buh she go know who is me now." Her intentions were to prove that she was affluent, self-sufficient, in this world's goods. It was as though she was in a huge angry competition with the world around her. She had something to prove and she was proving it, but the funny thing was all she wanted to see was just the money piling up in the bank; to be proud of her accounts receivables, and yes, to keep piling up more.

After paying off for the cocoa estate, Neeta purchased half an acre on the Eastern Main Road just opposite to the Pacheco big house. Remnants of the old stables, storerooms, and drying houses were visible on the land she now owned. Supported by their faded, white-washed, buttress like pillars, the several metal frames and tracks on which the wheels of the cocoa house roofs rolled were still present in her backyard. Sometime later they were all gone; Neeta was quick to barter with people. The tracks were probably sold to the highest bidder.

Having sold her house on Oropouche Road, she decided to live in an old house she bought with the new parcel of land. This house was probably the quarters for some of the laborers during the era of the Santa Estrella Estate. Adjacent to the house was something like an old garage. It could have been the stable where horses were kept. With a "garage" to house a car she went straightway and bought the car of her dreams. Although she could not drive, she always wanted a *Hillman Minx Deluxe*, the car of her dreams. She had promised herself to get one and she got the car--for cash! The vehicle remained in the "stable" collecting dust. Quero drove it from time to time but was too busy driving his taxi and looking after many more things unknown to Neeta. Eventually Rolly, a friend of hers, started driving the vehicle to transport her to and from her cocoa estate.

From the looks of things, the nuances, and the way Rolly spoke with her, Jonjon believes that this person was more than just a friend. It seemed that this relationship was intimate. Jonjon surmised, as the Trinidadian saying goes: "There is something in the mortar beside the pestle." Neeta had a way of hiding her relationships as though everyone was blind. She suffered from "the head in the sand with the backside in full view" syndrome. Her ostrich like behavior did not leave anyone guessing. When asked, she would always say, "Nah, he is just ah friend."

Although there was indoor plumbing there was still no toilet in this old house. Neeta moved from her country house at Kowlessur Road to reside here while building a big new house on one of her adjacent lots. The new house went up with all the frills and flair, but after its completion, it just stood there for years. It was clear that she was waiting for some special moment in time to occupy the house. For whatever reason, she continued to live in the dirty, dark, creepy, and unfriendly looking "slave" house with its weathered white-washed Demerara windows.

In this old house there seemed to be an impasse between Neeta and Quero. Neeta had the money and the land. Quero also had some money and his taxi. To Jonjon it seemed as though both of them were waiting for a showdown. What was it, "Who will be the "last man standing?" The fight for the money, the house and all the land began in earnest. Quero was not as attentive to Neeta as he used to be. He knew she was ailing with some form of illness and he just waited like a Comodo Dragon to see when she would fall. There was a newly built house and pieces of valuable real estate to claim if she departed. To Jonjon it was amazing to see how money, house, and land trigger hate and greed between people who lived all their lives together. The story gets more interesting. Quero was playing it by air, and patient as an alligator on a river bank; he preyed on Neeta's illness.

From the type of wild bush teas she prepared, it was suspect that Neeta was probably suffering from diabetes and possibly high blood pressure. Wild *carraili* (balsam apple) bush tea, a herbal remedy known for its use by diabetics was one of the "medicines" she frequently ingested. To help her sleep, every night she would drink a cup of tea brewed from soursop leaves. It seemed that she was afraid or too proud to go visit the doctor. In those days, the public stigmatized diabetics. She was afraid of the stigma of having diabetes or "sugar" so she avoided medical guidance and secretly tried to contend with the disease by herself by drinking a boiled concoction of several different herbs. If people knew that someone had diabetes, their friends would hail out to them, "How yuh sweet so?" Quero himself did not visit the doctor. He seemed strong, up and ready to go. He was a man who thought that nothing could happen to him. Many people live in a zone of a false sense of security, and as the saying goes in Trinidad, "the mark will buss one day," meaning that everything will come to light one day. "Bussing mark," comes from the illegal game known as "Whe Whe" where people's nightly dreams and signs are categorized with numbers from one to thirty-six. Numbers are played each day in some abandoned or remote spot to avoid the police. On this secret turf is where the "banker," the man with the money, will "buss the mark" (reveal the number) and the payout decided. Today the game called "Play Whe" is a legal, government owned, gambling game in Trinidad and Tobago.

Extramarital affairs polluted the relationship between Neeta and Quero. Jonjon will not disclose who told him, but Quero had Asha, his "outside" woman and Neeta also had a more or less secretive affair with Quero's good friend, Massood. From what Jonjon witnessed, there could have been others who were involved with Neeta. Until recently, Jonjon never had a clue about Quero's affair, but Neeta's interest in Massood was as glaring as the noonday sun. There was a day when Jonjon was at home on Oropouche Road with Neeta when Massood came. That day she was preparing steamed breadfruit and stewed fish. The dish required Norwegian cooking butter. She quickly welcomed Massood and then dispatched Jonjon to go purchase a pound of Norwegian cooking butter. Jonjon ran off and walked as fast as he could to Ramroop's grocery on the Eastern Main Road. He asked for the Norwegian cooking butter, paid the grocer, and trotted off back to Neeta's.

Neeta was astonished to see how quickly Jonjon returned. Apparently he returned too quickly so she made up some story that this was not the type of butter she wanted and sent him back forthwith to Ramroop's grocery. Jonjon was sensible enough to understand that she wanted a little more time and space with Massood. When Jonjon arrived, Massood's car was still parked under the house. To prevent any "disturbance" Jonjon went next door to his aunt's house and waited until Massood left. His cousins next door knew exactly what was going on because their *macometer* antennae were quite elevated. Their *mauvais langue* (badmouthing) about Neeta reached a crescendo during such moments. When Jonjon walked up the back steps the back door was locked--so strange. When Neeta was at home, the top section of the back door was usually left open for the cool breezes. Why was it closed today? Neeta could not hide her affair with Massood.

Meetings with Massood became even more intense when she went to live at Kowlessur Road. There were times when she would go off to the Manzanilla Beach with Massood and leave Boon and Jonjon at the country house. Sometimes both Jonjon and Boon would go along with them to the beach. Neeta would never go into the water. She would sit in the car with Massood until Jonjon and Boon were finished with their sea bathing. While Neeta was doing her thing, Quero was also engaged in his very own affair.

By this time, Jonjon was only looking in from the side. He did not interfere with Neeta's business. Rumor had it that she had amassed a huge amount of wealth, as much as TTD300,000 in one bank, TTD50,000 in another, and TTD16,000 in another bank. Her net worth after the building of the new house could have been anywhere in the vicinity of TTD3.5 million. Neeta had money and she was not about to share it with anybody. Moreover, she was not giving any charity to any church, but Neeta was a troubled woman. Neeta had dreams and three times she came to relate to Jonjon the import of her dreams. She constantly dreamt that she was crossing a bridge under which crystal water flowed. At one time she related that she was crossing the same bridge and someone on the other side of the bridge was calling out with outstretched arms to her to come over. Neeta felt a bit of trepidation because of these dreams and she reasoned that she should be baptized in a river. For a short period, Neeta could be seen attending the Evangelical Church on Ojoe Road in Sangre Grande, but her eyes showed discomfort. Jonjon told her that it would be best for her to get baptized but because of her money, Neeta hesitated. She kept saying, "I eh paying no pastor, priest, or pundit." She refused baptism because she did not want to give anything to any church. Tenaciously she clutched to her money.

From extremely good sources, the story is told that Quero had fallen in love with Asha since he was a young man. It is possible he had to hide his love for Asha from his family because of their religious beliefs. Asha was not a Muslim, and as we know, Quero's father was a respected imam in the village. They continued their secret affair until Asha was given to another man. Quero felt the hurt, but his love for Asha was never extinguished. Asha and her husband lived closed to Quero father's house. Domestic violence was one factor in Asha's life. Her life became hard and difficult. Quero could only look with pity upon her. Asha was his love and all he wanted for her was happiness. It was sad for Quero when he heard her screams everyday while her husband wickedly beat her. He beat her even more because he felt that she still loved Quero. Eventually she would get away from his wicked hands and run over to hide under Quero's house, and Quero would be there with open arms to welcome her. The drama between Quero, Asha, and her husband went on for many years until Asha ran away for good. Quero lost his love, and although he got married to Neeta, the tender moments he shared with his first love remained riveted in his mind. He became restless as a caged lion and began his quest to find Asha.

As a taxi driver, Quero met with many people from all walks of life. Talk would ensue between passengers and Quero would sometimes join in to give his two cents worth. Somehow he found himself deep in some talk about his "woman" and one thing rolled into another...the dominoes came crashing down until someone told him that he thought that Asha lived in Carapo, a little village south of the O'Meara Road junction in the Borough of Arima. He hastened to investigate the information and directions he received. Quero was not disappointed. His mission to find Asha was rewarded. There she was, a little older but still glorious and precious to him; lost but now found. Renewing their love for each other, Quero started visiting Asha on a daily basis. A couple years would fly by with Asha giving birth to their two children, a boy and a girl. Quero's mind was now occupied with Asha and his two children, but Neeta was still in his way. He did not want Neeta now. Jonjon could now visualize and comprehend why there was so much cussing and fighting between Neeta and Quero. It is clear the Neeta could not bear children and she knew that Quero had an affair with a woman somewhere. What she didn't know was that he had children with Asha.

Jonjon was now a grown man and his preference for common or yard fowl eggs was no exception. Many people in Trinidad prefer common fowl eggs above farm-raised eggs. Neeta was still raising chickens and invariably had a good supply of these eggs. One day he went up to Sangre Chiquito to ask Neeta for a dozen eggs. To him, Neeta looked pale, weakened, lonely, possessed of something that he could not nail down. Something was wrong and she was not speaking much; she looked distant. Her gait was just a shuffle, not as brisk as she used to be. The house was dark, dreary, and lifeless. Her face and arms were daubed with some kind of white and blue stuff that Jonjon couldn't figure out. Was it some ritual she was doing? Was she practicing some kind of obeah? Her mind seemed to be elsewhere. Some strange thing was happening to her. Neeta was not as collective as before. Her mental state left much to be desired. She had this weird stare that Jonjon never saw previously. This was not the Neeta he knew. She brought out the eggs and set them on the table. After a little chit-chat with her he took up the eggs to leave. Neeta turned to him and said, "Yuh have six dollars fuh mih fuh dem eggs yuh know." Jonjon looked at her and wondered if she really said that. "What? Six dollars?" was his reply. "I thought that you were giving me these eggs," he quipped. She continued, "Well, ah have tuh buy crack corn fuh di fowl and dem yuh know." Jonjon could not believe his ears. "Keep those eggs! I don't want them anymore. I prefer to go elsewhere!" he retorted. He looked at Neeta, his godmother, and thought about what she did to him, all his labor as a child, his pain and suffering in the cocoa field, and all the inconveniences he withstood to help

Neeta. Now she wanted to exact a six dollar payment from him for twelve eggs. Jonjon just couldn't believe that she was really charging him for the eggs. Her attitude was reprehensible! What a travesty! What a mean old lady! Once more, Neeta was true to form and saw the opportunity to make six dollars and her focus did not waver. She was stingy; she had not changed. Neeta was a miser and she preferred to die like that. She tried to smile when Jonjon was leaving but there was no return smile. Jonjon knew it was the last time he would visit her.

Time passed. Jonjon was grown and now a husband and father. He had stopped visiting Neeta until one day someone came to him and said that Neeta wanted to see him urgently. Jonjon could not have spared the time to go and look for Neeta. In fact, he did not acquiesce to her invitation. He reasoned that she knew where he lived and if she wanted to see him she should make the effort. Neeta had a car and she had a driver. Neeta was one to save gas. Every penny must be spent to benefit her. Then Jonjon heard the sad news; Neeta had died.

How Neeta died is a story in itself; somewhat mysterious, somewhat questionable. The reports about her death are vague, but still provoke much thought. Some say that nothing happens before its time. Taking the statement with a "pinch of salt," Neeta's death, it seems, happened because she did not get the required medical attention that she needed at a specific moment. The theory bandied about in her immediate neighborhood was that Quero dilly-dallied to provide the necessary care on the night when Neeta suddenly fell ill. Rolly, Neeta's alleged "boyfriend," told Jonjon that he could not understand why Quero dragged his heels to call the ambulance. Jonjon heard that Neeta was on the floor frothing. Neeta was plump and a little on the heavy side. Quero did not call the neighbors for help to lift Neeta into his car. Why? Rolly hinted that he felt that there was something fishy about the whole incident surrounding Neeta's passing. Quero acted as though he could not do any better. Apparently, Neeta went into a coma. According to Rolly, Neeta was frothing from the mouth when at long last the ambulance came. Neeta died on her way to the hospital. Rolly wondered if Quero was buying time before he called for help. It is possible that Quero wanted to make sure that Neeta arrived at a point of no return. Did Quero orchestrate the activities surrounding Neeta's death? Did she commit suicide? Was it a homicide? Many are the questions but there are no immediate answers.

Quero's reluctance to provide the much needed assistance that Neeta required could have been laced with the "opportunity" to eliminate her once and for all. This was his chance and he wasn't going to blow it. He was not going to let Neeta's wealth slip from his grasp. Everything Neeta owned fell into Quero's lap, the money, the new house, the cocoa estate, the car. It would seem that Quero, Asha, and their two children would be set for a life of bliss, living happily ever after. This is the type of story that underpins great movies; such intrigue.

Quero and Asha moved into the newly built mansion; the house that Neeta had hoped to occupy for the rest of her days. Without a doubt, Neeta had all the money and everything she needed to enjoy a good old age, at least so she thought. So many of us believe that we have our lives in our hands and that tomorrow belongs to us. Neeta didn't live to enjoy one black cent of her earnings. The cocoa and coffee beans she stole, and those she struggled to scrape up from the floor of the cocoa field which she converted to pennies, just flew past her. Despite her great wealth, she died in a squalid, dark, dank, and dreary old weather-beaten house; indeed, indeed, a fool and his money are soon parted. The wealth was still there, Neeta just left it.

At her funeral ceremony, no tears were shed, no eulogy given. In the cheapest of coffins she lay in the church, so few in attendance, and Quero was busy to get her into the ground. In the church, Jonjon, the only member of his family in attendance just sat there staring at the altar. He did not feel any sadness; without any fanfare, Neeta had come and gone, like a raindrop on hot asphalt. She had just sizzled away. Jonjon could still hear the sound of the huge cold clods of earth that came into contact with the coffin as the gravediggers hurriedly covered up the grave. A few wreaths were laid. Neeta was put to rest and the few witnesses at the graveside quietly walked away. What a life! The Cocoa Woman was no more, gone to her eternal rest.

After the dirge, Quero probably wallowed in glee; his ship had come in. His camels and dromedaries had come from afar, laden with gold and silver. Neeta was gone for good and he was now monarch of all he surveyed. The house was silent, no more "cuss outs" and displays of disgust. The exchange of invectives ceased. There seemed to be "peace in the valley." Quero must have thought to himself that all would be well from here onwards. He must have reasoned that he could now live it up; the money, the house, the car, the land were now his, but nature has a way of defying the best of plans. Two years later, Quero felt a sharp pain in his chest while he was cutting grass in the front yard of his mansion. Coronary thrombosis took its toll on Quero. Jonjon heard that Quero could not even make it up the stairs of his new house. He did not live long enough to really enjoy the money, the cocoa estate, the land, the house, and the car. Asha and her two little children inherited all that was derived from someone else's labor. Not only did Asha inherit the wealth, she inherited all the sentiments that went into creating the wealth, the pain, suffering, and discomfort of others who slaved in the cocoa field; all wrapped up in the bundle of wealth that the Cocoa Woman slaved, stole, struggled, and sacrificed to acquire.

In Jonjon's mind, it looked unfair that Asha and her children, without a day of toil and struggle, came into great wealth. Maybe that's the way the world works. It's all about the twists and turns of fate. Some people come into the right place at the right time. Jonjon wonders, did Neeta have any last thoughts as she lay helpless on the floor of her house? What was going through her mind as she studied all she worked for and fought the world to get? Did she have any thoughts at all? Life is a passing parade, there are actors, and there are onlookers. After a while Jonjon became an onlooker. He had nothing to say to Neeta or Quero. In fact, Quero still charged Jonjon his taxi fare for taking him to Port of Spain. Quero and Neeta found their enjoyment, pleasure, and excitement in just making money. They could not care whom they used and abused. That was not their business. Their business was to extract as much as they could get from whomsoever they could. They did not have a clue that life is so much more interesting when others are treated with respect, compassion, and love. There are maxims contained in the Vedas, two of which all of us will do well to remember: "All accumulation will end in loss. All rising will end in fall."

As far as Jonjon is concerned, Neeta understood life as nothing more than grinding work and a restless, miserable, unstoppable urge to create wealth without taking a moment to smell the roses. All that she sought to smell was the cocoa she harvested. In turn, she also smelled like cocoa mingled with sweat; the cocoa took full control of her. It was in her blood. She did not believe in relaxation. Having some pure fun was absent from her mentality. She saw life as a desperate moment to work, to make more money. She never traveled. Everything she did was to earn another dollar. Her salvation was money, every cent of it! What was her purpose in life? In Jonjon's mind, Neeta emerged as the embodiment of stinginess and greed. It is quite likely that she was born to be a tight-fisted and miserly Cocoa Woman. There was no delay in her metamorphosis. The funny thing is that the chickens are still clucking and scratching around, and of course, laying everywhere in the bushes. Sadly, no one is there to collect the eggs. The cocoa and coffee trees in Kowlessur Road are still growing and producing. Who is taking care of them?

GLOSSARY

CHAPTER 1

Cocoa Panyols— people who look like those of Spanish or Portuguese (fair-skinned) extract called *payol* in Trinidad and Tobago.

cracker-dull-- a small sharp steel blade about 8-12 inches long fitted with a short, cloth-wound, wooden handle

cuatro—small four-stringed instrument derived from the Portuguese cavaquinho; the national instrument of Venezuela

flot—empty cocoa beans that will float in water

kashema— Sugar apple, (*Annona squamosa*)

la peau-- uncleaned broken cocoa pods lying underneath a pile of fresh cocoa beans

louchet—a metal digger consisting of a flat blade three to four inches wide, ten to 12 inches long to which a long wooden handle is affixed

paranderos—a group of four or five men and sometimes a couple women who go from house to house to parang at Christmastime.

passé—past the prime; faded or aged, from old French "passer" to pass.

patois—broken French

poinyah—machete or cutlass

pommerac—Common names : Malay apple, mountain apple, otaheite apple (*Syzgium malaccense*), a pear shaped fruit with red skin and white flesh

pommecythere—June plum, golden apple (*Spondias dulcis*, syn. *Spondias cythere*)

rum shop—a pub; a gathering place for people who consume alcoholic beverages

Sangre Chiquito—little blood (Spanish)

Sangre Grande—big blood (Spanish)

CHAPTER 2

chulha—an earthen fireside that is normally constructed outside of the dwelling

"dey pores raise"—colloquial expression for the formation of goosebumps when frightened

juking dong—the act of bringing down an animal or object from its perch with the use of a sharpened lance or rod *jumbie*—ghost, apparition, zombie, spirit

lost vine—Trinidadian folklore mentions "lost vine" as a type of liana that grows in the rainforest there. Legend has it that treading on this vine results in being forever lost in the forest.

manicou— the name assigned to the opossum found in Trinidad (*Didelphis marsupialis insularis*)

social—In Trinidadian culture, the word "social" is used here in the sense meaning anti-social, high-brow, or uppity in behavior

CHAPTER 3

amchar—any unripe fruit chopped dried and preserved in mustard oil. Green mango, chalta, pommecythere (June plum) and other sour fruit are used to make amchar

belna— rolling pin (normal spelling in Hindi is *belan*)

bhagi—cooked spinach or dasheen (*Colocasia esculenta*) leaves with garlic, onion, hot pepper, salt, and coconut milk

Black Maria—the police vehicle used for transporting prisoners

blood hole—a location in the gayelle where bois men go to bleed out

bois flot— a tropical tree that produces a soft brownish fiber used for stuffing pillows and mattresses (*Ochroma pyramidale*)

bowray—the act of dipping and picking up chunks of meat or vegetable with a small controllable piece of roti

Blue—a product dissolved in clean water to rinse white clothes

caca mange—filth eater (Patois)

callaloo— a soup like dish created from young dasheen (*Colocasia esculenta*) leaves, young ochro pods, coconut milk, and seasonings

caray—the position a stickman takes in "pelting a bois" or defending himself from a hit with the opponents bois (wood)

chalta—Elephant apple (*Dillenia indica*)... a large hard fruit with a bitter-sour taste used in East Indian cuisine for curries, jam, and jellies. It is often mixed with coconut and spices to make chutneys and amchar

chawki—a flat round smooth piece of seasoned non-poisonous wood about 12-14 inches in diameter on which the loi is rolled out with a belna

cocoa estate—cocoa plantation, cocoa land, mixed cultivation of cocoa, coffee, bananas, citrus, etc

couyenard— unlearned, awkward, ignorant, nonsensical, stupid, and in Trinidadian dialect, "dotish," "couyon"

Crix biscuit—a small round soda plain or multigrain cracker manufactured by the Bermudez Biscuit Company in Trinidad

dabla—a long wooden spatula

dhalgotni—a type of multipronged swizzle stick for swizzling dhal.

dhalpourri roti—an East Indian white flour flatbread stuffed with pre-cooked seasoned ground dhal (yellow split peas), fried on a griddle

dog rice—broken rice grains sold as pet food

doo-doo—sweetheart, darling, lover, honeybunch

Eid-ul-Fitr—Islamic holiday celebrated at the sighting of the crescent moon after the month of Ramadan

gambage—posturing; sizing up someone with deft moves; making a play or approach to fight

gayelle—an informal stage or arena; an area/space for challenge and contests, for example in Stick fighting and Cock fighting

genneh—in patois, maybe an adaptation from the French "je nais" meaning *I am not* or simply, *out of place.*

gotay—to swizzle or stir vigorously to crush something into a liquid.

imam—an Islamic cleric

kalinda—a type of dance-like martial art sometimes acted out with the use of staves that came with the arrival of Africans who were sold into slavery

loi—a small round smooth ball of flour dough

macaroni pie— a baked dish or casserole comprised of macaroni, eggs, seasonings, milk, and cheese

mamagism—the use of flattery and untruth to deceive someone

mon chere—patois for "my dear"

najaar—a condition believed to occur when someone gives another the evil eye. Many say that the receiving person suffers weakness, anorexia, lassitude for no apparent reason

"pelt a good bois"—making a good hit with a bois or wood used in stick fighting; this expression could also be associated with male sexual prowess

posey—night pot, "'tensil"

Poui tree—a flowering tree with bright yellow flowers appearing during the dry season in Trinidad (*Tabebuia serratifolia*)

sada roti—a type of flatbread made from bleached wheat flour, salt, and baking powder.

sannay—mixing rice with bhagi, talkaree, meat, sauce before eating…normally done with the right hand in Islamic culture

"so-and-so"— the euphemism for four-letter curse words

soucouyant— a shape-shifting Caribbean folklore character who appears as a reclusive old woman by day. By night, she strips off her wrinkled skin and puts it in a wooden mortar

talkaree— a vegetable or meat side dish made with enough sauce for dipping roti

taria—a large earthenware, brass or enameled plate with a slightly raised side

tawah—a flat circular metal griddle used for cooking flatbreads such as roti

CHAPTER 4

"ah lil blague"—a little bit of old talk, chit-chat

belle femme garcon—patois: good looking woman my boy

bodi—asparagus bean, yard long bean or snake bean (*Vigna unguiculata* subsp. sesquipedalis) *bridle road*—unpaved secondary road used mainly for draught animals

carat—palm fronds

chupons—young straight unproductive shoots that sometimes emerge in clusters from the root or base of a cocoa tree

common fowl—yard fowl, cage free hard fowl raised around the house

crapaud—frog (French)

crookstick— a tool made from a branch with a 90 degree hook at the end (most times a coffee branch) that aids in the cutting of grass with a swiper. This tool allows clearance for the fall of the swiper blade at the base of the bush.

cushion—the pad or raised area on the trunk of a cocoa tree from which flowers emerge.

cuss bud—one who is a constant user of curse words or "four-letter words" and/or invectives in Trinidad.

cutlassing— brushcutting; clearing an area of brush with the use of a swiper.

"dah who you?"—Who are you?

drainerman—one who digs drains on cocoa plantations

fever grass—lemon grass (*Cymbopogan citratus*)

frere—from the French creole or patois meaning *brother* which shows that Grenada was at one time a French colony

kamayung—nice, good, clean brushing cutlass work

maco—one who is addicted to minding other people's business; used also to describe something that is huge or of immense proportion, such as in this statement, "That is a *maco* piece of yam you have there."

macometer—a cerebral *device*, especially unique to Trinidadians that facilitates detection, retention, and repetition of other people's affairs

mauvais langue—badmouthing people and the happenings of the day

mathias—bad quality workmanship

paytayed—watched closely without the other party knowing

peton—support, a kind of third foot; getting a good footing to do something strenuous

roundeer—to clean around the trunk of a tree; to free the tree of weeds

sagaboy—a smooth talking, fancy dressing young man who seeks the affection of several women

sapate´—a type of heavy clayey soil normally found where cocoa is grown.

seim—a vining bean normally grown on a trellis in the backyards or on fences in Trinidad (*Dolichos lablab*)

shadon beni—a wild pungent herb known also as culantro or bandania used in seasoning preparations, especially for fish preparations; also used in folk medicine (*Eryngium foetidum*)

shandilay—a very bitter herb used in folk medicine preparations for coughs and colds (*Leonotis nepetifolia*) *tapia*—adobe, mud mixed with cow's dung and finely chopped grass to make a paste for plastering

white man—reference to the owner of hundreds of acres of land. Such owners were white-skinned or of French extract.

CHAPTER 5

agouti—a small rodent hunted in Trinidad for its meat (*Dasyprocta leporina*)

aloo—Irish potato

bodaage— the border, leeway, or transition zone between boundaries

bounjay—toss up meat or other material in hot seasoned oil

Brasso—a type of polish used for shining brass

breadfruit—a large seasonal fleshy fruit relative to breadnut (chataigne) and Jackfruit that tastes like bread when roasted (*Artocarpus altilis*)

cassava pone—a baked, sweet, pudding-like dessert made from grated cassava (*Manihot esculenta*) and grated coconut

channa—chick peas, garbanzo beans

chataigne—breadnut (*Artocarpus camansi*)

cobwebbing—removal of spider webs

coconut bake—a type of flatbread with the essential ingredient being grated coconut. In country living the bake was cooked on a chulha inside an iron pot under which was a tiny bit of glowing coals while on top of the cover of the pot there would be a strong blazing fire (*fire on top, fire below*)

common fowl—yard fowl, non-pedigree chickens raised in the yard around the home

crapaud—frog (French)

"down below"—refers to the city and/or unfamiliar with country life. In Trinidad, "down below" could mean Port of Spain or San Fernando.

flambeau—open-flame light made with a wick immersed in a bottle of kerosene

gamalot grass—a grass that is usually unwanted in a cocoa field (*Chaetochloa sulcata*)

lappe—spotted paca, a ground-dwelling, herbivorous rodent hunted for its meat in Trinidad (*Cuniculus paca*)

lime—shoot the breeze, hang out

lorha—a hard, smooth oval stone

mapipire—a type of venomous viper extant in Trinidad

moubeh tree—hogplum tree (*Spondias dulcis*)

"yuh cyar play mas if yuh 'fraid powder"—you cannot be in the game if you fear the game. If you are a masquerader you must tolerate the talcum powder that others throw on you

paytayed—look at something closely with intent of discovery

pisay—grind, crush with a stone

pot hound—a breed of dog without pedigree

raebuk—the few ripe cocoa pods normally harvested during the summer

ryo—plants or canes of the Dracaena species used for identifying boundaries

samblay—possibly from the French "assemble" to bring together into a group

sil—a large, hard, flat and heavy rock with a recess to accommodate the lorha.

sohari leaf or kashiboo leaf—a wild plant with leaves like that of the banana plant used as a "tray" or receptacle for food at East Indian weddings and religious gatherings (*Calathea lutea*)

tom-tom—green plantains pounded and formed into a bolus

CHAPTER 6

chile--child

chunkay—to pour hot garlic infused oil into a pot of dhal or other food

cocoyea—dried coconut palm leaf midribs

bois canot tree—Trumpet tree (*Cecropia peltata*)

bun-bun—the charred remnants at the bottom of the pot.

farse—inquisitive, a *maco* is normally farse

floneer—to raise a bird cage high up into the tree top by means of a rope

kalchool—a metal ladle

karat—a circular pad constructed from dried banana leaves or cloth

kashema—sugar apple (*Annona reticulata*)

peerha—small, low, one-seater bench, normally made from wood

pelau—a brown mixture of rice, pigeon peas, carrots, fresh coconut milk, chicken and seasonings

rabo—a flat piece of cedar wood about one inch thick, four inches wide, 12 inches long affixed to a thin strong six-foot long bamboo pole to manipulate cocoa beans while drying.

tabanca—a state of longing, brooding over a lost love, unrequited love

BRIEF NOTES ABOUT THE AUTHOR

A T THE BEGINNING of the 1959/1960 school year, Johnny Coomansingh began his primary school training at the Sangre Grande Seventh Day Adventist Elementary School. Under the watchful eyes and tutelage of Elias A. Toussaint, the principal, and Earlington McClatchie, his Standard One and Standard Five teacher, he succeeded at passing the Common Entrance Examinations (CE). His success at the Common Entrance Exams provided for "free" education and placement at Northeastern College, Sangre Grande where he spent roughly six years in pursuit of the ordinary level, Cambridge University, General Certificate of Education (GCE).

In the summer of 1972, after hearing of his exploits at Northeastern College, he was called to teach at Bates Memorial High School (BMHS) of Seventh Day Adventists. At BMHS he was scheduled to teach Health Science/Human & Social Biology and Mathematics (algebra, arithmetic, geometry) to forms four and five, New Mathematics to forms one, two, and three, Integrated Science in forms one, two, and three, and as the form master for form three, he taught Scripture (Christian Beliefs) in form three. After three years, he was also teaching Regional Geography, and English composition in form five as part of students' preparation for the GCE. His other school duties included Sports Master,

Health Educator, and Dean of Discipline, a full plate for a very young man. He was just 18 years old when he started.

While at BMHS, he pursued and passed the Associate of the College of Preceptors (A.C.P), a teaching degree at the teacher training level. At the end of his fourth year, he accepted a bursary to attend the Eastern Caribbean Institute of Agriculture and Forestry (ECIAF) where he read for a two-year Diploma in Agriculture and succeeded with credit. Although he was trained to teach agriculture, he was sent back to teach math and science at BMHS. After two more years, the teaching arrangement became unsuitable for him and so he ended his duties at BMHS. Note that after his success at the A.C.P he went in pursuit of the Licentiate of the College of Preceptors (L.C.P) which he completed in 1990, the equivalent of a bachelor's degree in education. His thesis for this degree was *"The Informal Approach to Farmer Education in Trinidad and Tobago."* In the LCP process, he was also awarded a Certificate in Psychology from the College of Preceptors, now known as the College of Teachers in London.

Following his tenure at BMHS he landed a job as an Agricultural-Assistant in the Ministry of Agriculture. After spending eight months involved with the management of Africanized honey bees and honey production in the Apiaries Department of the Extension Division, he was called to take up a new office in the Publications Unit of the Information and Training Department of the ministry. He was placed in the Publications Unit because of his deep interest in media and communication arts. In the unit he worked on the production of agricultural career packages for high school students, farmers' bulletins, agricultural cartoons, slogans, brochures, slide production, *AgriNews* journalism, graphic designs, agricultural exhibitions, Home Gardening/4-H, photography, lithography, portable display units, agricultural education, farmer training, transfer of technology, and public relations. Here he stayed for nine and a half years. At one time he also served as Press Officer/Public Relations for the Minister of Agriculture, St. Clair, Port of Spain.

Seeing that there was little hope for promotion in the Ministry of Agriculture, he applied for the position of Assistant Public Relations Officer in the Trinidad and Tobago Petroleum Company (TRINTOPEC) in 1990. Although he arrived late for his first interview, he was eventually selected as the most qualified candidate from a field of 127 applicants. He stayed with TRINTOPEC until the merger between TRINTOPEC and the Trinidad and Tobago Oil Company (TRINTOC). In view of his role/responsibility in The Petroleum Company of Trinidad and Tobago (PETROTRIN) the new oil company as a Corporate Communications Officer, he pursued a Bachelor of Technology (BT) at Andrews University extension campus at Caribbean Union College and graduated in August 1996. Around this moment in his experience, upheavals in his family life saw the family breaking apart, and with the resolve to still make sure his two boys had a fighting chance at life, he decided to take voluntary retirement and migrate to the United States. In 1996 he left PETROTRIN with the express intention of becoming a university professor.

It was a very sad and painful moment in his life having to leave Trinidad, but in the USA he was welcomed by his relatives and professors in the state of Kansas. His educational advancement in the United States of America was relentless. Capturing a seat every day in class at Fort Hays State University in Hays, Kansas, he graduated in record time with a Master of Science (MS) in Communication. At Fort Hays State he accepted a part-time position as a graduate teaching assistant and taught two sections of the *Fundamentals of Oral Communication*. Not wasting any time, he followed through to Kansas State University (KSU) where he succeeded in obtaining both a Master of Arts (MA) in Geography and a Doctor of Philosophy (PhD) in Geography. His thesis for the MA was *"Trinidad Carnival as an Amalgam of Borrowed Cultural Elements."* In 2001, he was awarded the distinction of "Distinguished Graduate Teaching Assistant" in geography at KSU, and president of Gamma Theta Upsilon—Beta Psi Chapter of the International Geographical Society at the university. His focus in the field of geography was centered on cultural geography, tourism, and rural economic development.

In 2003, before he even completed his PhD, he was offered a position to teach *World Tourism Geographies, Fundamentals of Tourism Management, Cultural Geography, World Regional Geography,* and *Geographical Perspectives* at Missouri State University (MSU) in Springfield, Missouri. During his "sojourn" at MSU he completed his PhD dissertation, titled: *Commodification and Distribution of the Steelpan as a Conflicted Tourism Resource* and graduated in 2005, one year ahead of time. He spent two years at Missouri State after which he went to Minot State University, North Dakota where he became the Coordinator of the Geography Department in the Division of Social Science. There he taught a wide range of upper level geography courses including, *Political Geography, The Geography of Economic Behavior, Geographic Information Systems, Cultural Geography, World Tourism Geographies, Geography of the Caribbean, Geography of Africa, Geography of North America, Geography of Central Asia,* and *Geography of Latin America.* He also presented his research on the steelpan and other topics related to tourism at various conferences hosted in the USA and Canada.

He writes every day. He has admitted that at the nib of a pen he fights his wars and wins his battles. So far he has authored several journal articles, poems, two book chapters, and published four books: *Show Me Equality, Sweet and Sour Trinidad and Tobago, Seven Years on Adventist Street,* and *Cocoa Woman: a Narrative about Cocoa Estate Culture in the British West Indies.* He is presently working on two more books, an anthology titled: *"Silence is no Weapon,"* and *"Fifty Years After: Encounters, Incidents, Realities."* The peoples and culture of Trinidad and Tobago, and the Caribbean in general attract his attention.

Johnny Coomansingh
November, 2018